DETERMINING THE COLLEGE FOOTBALL PLAYOFF

WEIGHTED WINS, A BETTER APPROACH

RAY D. THEIS
AND MARK G. TERWILLIGER

NEWMAN SPRINGS PUBLISHING
320 Broad Street
Red Bank, NJ 07701

First originally published by Newman Springs Publishing 2021

ISBN 978-1-63692-890-6 (Paperback)
ISBN 978-1-63692-891-3 (Digital)

Printed in the United States of America

This book is dedicated to all fair-minded college football fans. Ray would like to dedicate it to David, Jay, Nick, Scott, Paula, and Megan. Mark would like to dedicate the book to Kelly, Adam, and Luke. Both authors would like to thank Tom Boger for his valuable feedback.

If lessons are learned in defeat, our team is getting a great education.

—Murray Warmath,
former Minnesota football coach

CONTENTS

CHAPTER 1

WHY CONSIDER ANOTHER SYSTEM?

*It wasn't right. I was watching every week, the com-
mittee sitting in a room and [deciding] this two-loss
team must be better than UCF because UCF is in
the American. Or this three-loss team must be better
than UCF.*

—Scott Frost,
former University of Central
Florida (UCF) football coach

Since NCAA Division I Football Bowl Subdivision is the only major
athletic entity that does not have a well-defined objective method of
selecting teams to participate in its playoffs, some thoughts and ideas
on how to improve the system are included in this book. Because of
the limited number of games played in a season, several teams with
identical records may be bunched together at the top of the heap.
When multiple teams finish their seasons with identical records, how
should the "best" team be determined?

In Major League Baseball, with its 162-game schedule, teams are allowed to work their way to the top of the standings for the right to participate in the playoffs. The National Basketball Association also has teams play enough games to emerge to the top of the standings in their respective divisions. In the National Football League, with fewer games, teams are often tied in the standings. In order to deal with this, a total of twelve tiebreakers are defined, with head-to-head being the first one employed and a flip of a coin serving as a last resort. A similar strategy is employed for several other NCAA sports across all divisions. The point is that most sports entities have a definitive method set before the season starts to determine the teams that will advance to the playoffs.

NCAA Division I Basketball uses a hybrid system to select the national championship participants. The "champion" of every conference, determined either by regular season standings or through a conference tournament, receives an automatic entry into the NCAA tournament. The remainder of the field is selected by a blue-ribbon selection committee, which also places all the participants into the tournament bracket. Since all conference tournament winners are included in the playoff brackets, it can be claimed that we have a true Division I basketball champion. While there is always some controversy over the final field selection and placement, there seems to be a reasonable level of satisfaction that the best teams end up making it to the Elite Eight.

To pattern itself after college basketball, the power structure of college football decided to adopt a process utilizing a selection committee to pick four teams for the playoffs. The controversy in selecting at large teams for the basketball brackets and the four best teams in football is amplified by politics. The political nature of committee work makes some voices more powerful than others, with subjectivity and individual opinions permeating the results. Biases and inconsistencies are inevitable from year to year. The current process has already displayed those characteristics.

The top level of college football in the United States is the NCAA Division I Football Bowl Subdivision (FBS). Known previously as Division I-A, the FBS consists of ten conferences and 130 schools, as of 2020. A lower NCAA division, known as Division I-AA until 2005, the Football Championship Subdivision (FCS) offers fewer scholarships, and the schools do not compete in the postseason bowl games. Of the 127 FCS teams, the top 24 compete in a playoff for the NCAA Division I Football Championship. Throughout the book, when we refer to non-Bowl Subdivision teams, we are referring to either an FCS or an NCAA Division II school.

The ten FBS conferences have informally been split into two classes. The Power Five includes the Atlantic Coast Conference (ACC), Big Ten Conference, Big 12 Conference, Pac-12 Conference, and Southeastern Conference (SEC). The Group of Five consists of the American Athletic Conference, Conference USA, Mid-American Conference, Mountain West Conference, and Sun Belt Conference. It's worth noting that there is also a group of seven independent FBS teams that do not belong to a conference.

This stratification of NCAA Division I Bowl Subdivision Football into the Power Five and Group of Five conferences introduces an added complication. The lack of support that the Group of Five conference teams have makes it virtually impossible for them to compete for the championship. In the past seven years, several Group of Five teams have had very successful seasons yet ended up receiving very little recognition. In the preseason polls, as well as in several ranking systems, it's difficult to find a Group of Five team. They have to gradually work their way into recognition. We believe that a system is needed that ignores all polls and instead starts with a level playing field and lets the win-loss records determine the weekly standings, much like other sports.

Media reports indicate that the "power brokers" of the College Football Playoff (CFP) are happy with the playoff system. In a 2018 interview on the *Paul Finebaum Show*, CFP executive director Bill Hancock defended the transparency of the selection committee, although criteria utilized in one instance was not the same in another instance. When pushed on the process being more transparent, Hancock argued it might compromise the integrity and candor of the committee.

"When we first created the playoff, we said the committee would be as transparent as possible. The threshold on transparency is candor. It's important to protect the candor in the room. We will continue to look for ways to be as transparent as possible while protecting the candor," Hancock said at that time.

It appears that what works for certain influential conferences (or teams) is the direction the discussion goes. While the inner circle may be happy with the process, the average fan is not as convinced that political influence stays out of the deliberations. Conference protectionism is apparent, and so is the Group of Five exclusion. One strong voice in a committee can lead a discussion, and financial considerations finish it. Strong financial outcomes always make the commissioners and university presidents happy. To Illustrate the disparity between Power Five conferences and Group of Five conferences, take a look at the following table:

Total Appearances in the College Football Playoffs							
Conferences	ACC	SEC	Big Ten	Big 12	Pac-12	Independents	Group of 5
Number of Appearances	8	8	5	4	2	2	0

Where does this leave the Group of Five conferences? Since the "eye test" and "style points" are heavily utilized by the media to influence the committee, teams from these conferences usually begin each year well down in the rankings and polls. They have to climb the ladder slowly as the season progresses to gain some recognition. Schematically, it is almost impossible for them to reach the top 4 even though they may be undefeated and present a "good résumé." As discussed in chapter 4, the 2017 season results provide a great example of power politics at work. If we are going to categorically exempt Group of Five teams from the playoffs, let's be honest and just call it a Power Five championship.

The selection committee should be replaced by a well-defined system that ensures that all teams in the Division I Bowl Subdivision have a chance at the championship. Teams are then chosen for the playoffs by their standing in the system. A system that has been well tested with forty years of data has been developed. This system has shown remarkable reliability, validity, and general fan agreement, as supported by the polls. The system offers complete transparency as it removes the politics, removes biases, provides consistent results from year to year, and in general, includes teams that earned their spot without political influence. Built into the system is a strength-of-schedule factor that credits teams that play strong teams. The only thing that matters is winning and defeating other teams with strong records. The standings in the system are based totally on wins and the strength of those wins. Losses are also weighted in a fair and consistent manner based on the wins and losses of the teams involved.

The current CFP system has little transparency, consistency, reliability, or validity and leaves the fans uninformed about the factors in the discussions. These characteristics make the current system unsatisfactory and unacceptable to the average college football fan. To the college football fan, fairness is paramount.

CHAPTER 2

COLLEGE FOOTBALL RANKING SYSTEMS

There should be eight. If you win your conference, there's five of us. You win that, you're in. Then the Central Floridas of the world, the Boises of the world, who are 12-0, or whoever is the highest-ranked team, they should be in.

—Mike Gundy,
Oklahoma State football coach,
when asked how many teams should
be in the college football playoffs

The declaration of a college football champion has been a source of controversy for many years. From 1869 until 1998, a "mythical" champion was designated by the media. Media organizations such as the Associated Press (AP), United Press International (UPI), Football Writers Association of America (FWAA), *USA Today*/CNN, and others promoted various champions. Beginning in 1869, an organization called the National Championship Foundation (NCF) named the champion. Initially, Ivy League schools, especially Harvard, Yale, and Princeton, dominated, with Yale being named champion sixteen times, including its final title in 1927. As college football became more popular and spread across the country, schools like Michigan, Penn State, Pittsburgh, Georgia Tech, and LSU started to gain championship recognition.

As football grew and gained notoriety, the number of organizations that declared a champion in college football also increased. In 1919, four different organizations named four different college football champions. It wasn't until 1936 that the AP became the dominant media outlet and named Minnesota the national champion. The AP served in that capacity until about 1950, when UPI became involved, followed closely by FWAA and the National Football Foundation (NFF). These four media outlets were heavily involved until 1998, when the Bowl Championship Series (BCS) was created. The BCS was a combination of polls and computer rating systems. The BCS formula was an attempt to create a more standardized method of determining the champion since the polling method created so much controversy. The BCS formula was intended to match the two best teams in a playoff. There were several adjustments to the BCS formula in the early years, with some computer models added and others deleted.

Because of the complexity of most of the computer systems, football fans did not readily accept the process. It lacked the transparency for the average football fan to understand and digest. Most of the computer systems involved mathematical formulas and calculations that required a knowledge of advanced mathematics. This lack of understanding and transparency was probably responsible for the system to be abandoned in 2014 in favor of a College Football Playoff (CFP) selection committee. This selection committee was charged with the task of determining the four best teams in college football and matching them in a four-team playoff.

To follow the evolution of a college football champion, we have gone from a process of having the media declare a national champion to a process of having a hybrid system of computers and polls to having a selection committee choose four teams for a playoff. The AP was the most recognized media outlet and was comprised of about six-ty-five voters who covered college football. The CFP selection committee is comprised of thirteen members, most of whom are former high-profile football coaches, athletic directors, and commissioners.

Controversies in the Poll Years

The AP was the only poll that declared a national champion from 1936 to 1949. However, in 1950, the United Press International (UPI), along with the AP, declared the same team the champion. By 1954, the FWAA had joined the parade and declared its own champion. Again, there was agreement among the polls until 1954, when both UCLA and Ohio State received the recognition of champion. Since 1936, which is usually considered the beginning of the modern era of college football champions, that disagreement in 1954 was the first. The NFF added its ranking system in 1959, leading to four different outlets declaring a national champion. In the modern era, there were twelve years in which two different teams were declared national champion. Additionally, three different teams were declared national champion in both 1964 and 1970. In the polling systems, regional biases were prominent and skewed the results of the polls. This muddied the water in terms of who really was the best team in college football. In 1990, Colorado got the nod for being national champion by the AP, and Georgia Tech got the nod in the Coaches Poll. In 1991, Washington and Miami (Florida) again shared the title by split polls. These splits by the polls amplified the push for a more definitive method of determining the national champion. As a result, a bowl coalition was formed to hopefully match up the best two teams. Since conferences had ties to various bowls, however, a perfect matchup was not always possible. In 1997, Michigan and Nebraska shared the title since both undefeated teams won their bowl games. Michigan was tied to the Rose Bowl, and Nebraska linked to the Orange Bowl by conference affiliation, thus preventing the tiebreaking matchup.

Weaknesses of the BCS Formula

The first attempt at a more standardized method of determining the national champion was the creation of the Bowl Championship Series (BCS) in 1998. It was formed by the commissioners of the Big East (now the American Athletic Conference), Atlantic Coast Conference, Big Ten, Big 12, Pac-10 (now the Pac-12), and Southeastern Conference. The initial BCS formula used two polls and three computer ranking systems to select the teams that would play in the championship game. The two polls used in that initial formula were the AP poll and the Coaches Poll, while the computer models that were used included the Sagarin rankings, the *New York Times* model, and the *Seattle Times* / Anderson & Hester model.

The BCS committee's discussion about the value of margin of victory led to early changes in the process. Both the *New York Times* (*NYT*) and Sagarin computer results had a margin of victory component, while the Seattle Times did not. The decision to remove the margin of victory from the computers that employed this measure led to the NYT computer model being dropped from the BCS formula. Sagarin agreed to remove that component from his formula and had two rankings that were published in the *USA Today*. Since the Sagarin rankings were proprietary, it's not known exactly how the model was changed. This lack of transparency is one of the basic reasons that the BCS formula was not accepted by the average football fan.

After the *New York Times* was dropped from the formula, new groups were added. This included Billingsley, Massey, Rothman, Scripps-Howard, and later, Peter Wolfe and Wes Colley. The continual flux in the computer formula and the complexity of the mathematics involved turned off the average college football fan. The lack of transparency and unknown criteria utilized in the computers doomed the system.

With the end to the BCS era came the CFP, or College Football Playoff, committee. This committee was formed to have a group of football "experts" select the teams to play in a four-team playoff. The composition of the committee is made up of former high-profile coaches, athletic directors, conference commissioners, and former players. The composition of this group changes every few years.

Perceived Problems of CFP Committee

While the committee is no doubt composed of members of the highest integrity, human nature, being what it is, makes it extremely difficult to not be influenced by college affiliation. Although the committee has a recusal policy for close ties to universities, other connections also enter into the equation, and all are impossible to eliminate.

The criteria used by the CFP selection committee is also difficult to pin down. It appears to the average fan that what applies one year does not hold true the next. One thing that appears obviously true is that you have to be a member of a Power Five conference to be included in the top 4. In the development of the BCS Formula, the margin of victory became a big issue, with some computers being dropped because of margin of victory. Now the media has promoted the idea of "eye test" and "style points," which implies running up the score. In many respects, we have come full circle from the polls to CFP committee selection. To reflect on eye test and style points, in the 1960 World Series between the Pittsburgh Pirates and New York Yankees, the Yankees won three games by a combined 38–3 margin, while the Pirates won four games by combined scores of 24–17. Total runs scored: Yankees, 55; Pirates, 27. Who won the World Series? So much for the eye test and style points. When two of the best football teams meet, all that matters is who won. Running up the score on weak opponents is not good for the winning team and is not good for college football in general.

The politics of the selection committee is hard to overlook. The executive director of the CFP committee is supposedly the glue of the committee offering guidelines and criteria. The early criteria included strength of schedule, conference championships, team record, head-to-head matchups, injuries, and weather. Thinking about some of those items, we might ask, Does an injury to the water boy count, or does it have to be a five-star quarterback? When does the weather factor kick in? These two intangibles have been a part of college football from its inception. In the case of the weather, the two teams are playing on the same field, and may the best team win. It appears from the early discussion that these intangible factors were built in to provide wiggle room for the committee to arrive at a favorable conclusion.

The politics of the media is also very prominent. ESPN, a sponsor of the Southeastern Conference, is constantly touting the possibility of getting two teams from that conference in the playoffs. The ESPN commentators are frequently talking about the eye test and style points. College football is the only major sport that does not have a well-defined objective system for its playoffs. Professional football has a playoff system based on conference standings and a set of tiebreakers. Is this the next step for college football?

In the attempt to research the criteria utilized by the committee, only nebulous and capricious commonalities existed in the first four years of the committee's work. These commonalities were thus:

1. Reach Selection Sunday with one or fewer losses.
2. Defeat at least three teams ranked in the Selection Sunday's top 25.
3. Win at least six games against FBS teams that have a 0.500-plus record on Selection Sunday.
4. Win a Power Five conference championship.

While these may seem like reasonable standards, they were not always followed closely. In checking games schedule against FCS schools during the most recent season, SEC teams played fourteen games against FCS teams. The ACC scheduled thirteen games, the Pac-12 scheduled eight games, the Big 12 scheduled seven games, and the Big Ten scheduled only three FCS opponents. In some cases, the wins over FCS teams put an FBS team with a 5–6 record into the 0.500-plus category to help pad the qualifications for item 3 listed above.

CHAPTER 3

WHAT IS WEIGHTED WINS?

Always remember: Goliath was a 40-point favorite over David.

—Shug Jordan,
former Auburn football coach

The basic premise of weighted wins is one the average fan would readily accept. All wins are not equal. Defeating a highly successful team, one with a winning record, is more difficult than defeating an unsuccessful team, one with a losing record. Therefore, the system assigns a weight to each opponent. This weight is determined in a fair, unbiased, and systematic manner by considering a team's record and the records of its opponents. After the weights are assigned, teams accumulate weighted wins and weighted losses.

In this chapter, the weighted wins process will be explained. This includes describing the concepts of *initial weights* and *final weights*, as well as the overall *weighted wins* value that is used to create the standings for the system.

Criteria for Weighted Wins

The criteria for weighted wins are built on wins and the quality of those wins. Defeating a winning team adds to your *weight*, while losing to a losing team reduces your *weight*. The following criteria incorporate the logic of the system:

1. The initial weight (IW) of a team reflects its own record. All games against Bowl Subdivision teams and all losses to non-Bowl Subdivision teams are counted in determining IW.
2. The final weight (FW) of a team reflects the strength of schedule of that team based on the given conditions:
    A. Defeating a winning team *increases* the winning team's final weight.
    B. Defeating a losing team *does not increase* the winning team's final weight.
    C. Losing to a winning team *does not reduce* the losing team's final weight.
    D. Losing to a losing team *reduces* the losing team's final weight.
    E. Losing to a non-Bowl Subdivision team *reduces* the losing team's final weight.
3. In the weighted wins computing process for a given team's season, its *losses* are counted first.
4. Games against non-Bowl Subdivision teams do not count if a victory occurs; however, losses to non-Bowl Subdivision teams are penalized.
5. Because teams don't necessarily all play the same number of games, only ten games are counted toward the weighted wins (WW) in a regular eleven-game season. Even though most teams play more than ten games, the effectiveness of the system is not diminished by omitting games against one weaker team. This allows some crossover between Bowl Subdivision and other divisions. In the event of an

expanded schedule, if all top 10 teams have played twelve games, then eleven games could be calculated.

6. All games played throughout the season are treated equally. A quality team that defeats another quality team early in the season receives as much credit as a quality team that defeats another quality team late in the season. The season's ending record is what ultimately counts.

During the season, standings are determined by calculating the *initial weights* and *final weights* based on the games played up to that point.

Determining Weights: The Initial Weight

In sports, teams with a 0.500 winning percentage are considered average teams. Therefore, assigning a weight of 1.00 to a 0.500 team is the starting point for establishing the initial weight.

The initial weight (IW) is a reflection of a team's own record against all Division I Bowl Subdivision. The initial weight (IW) can be computed at any time during the season; it is an indication of a team's current record. The IW takes into consideration all games played against Bowl Subdivision teams. During the season, the initial weight for any team with the same number of wins and losses (0-0, 1-1, 2-2, 3-3, 4-4, 5-5) is 1.0. A team's IW changes each week as it accumulates wins and losses. At the end of a season, a team with a 6–6 record would have an initial weight of 1.00.

A team's IW is increased by 0.01 for each win more than the number of losses and decreases by 0.01 for each loss more than the number of wins. For example, a team with a 9–3 record would have an IW of 1.06 (six more wins than losses), while a team with a 3–8 record would have an IW of 0.95 (five more losses than wins). During the season, a team may have a 4–3 record and an initial weight of 1.01. If this team wins the following week, its record would be 5–3, with an IW of 1.02. At any time during the season, the initial weight is determined by the games it has played up to that point.

The following tables illustrate the initial weight for both eleven- and twelve-game seasons.

Record	IW	Record	IW
11-0	1.11	12-0	1.12
10-1	1.09	11-1	1.10
9-2	1.07	10-2	1.08
8-3	1.05	9-3	1.06
7-4	1.03	8-4	1.04
6-5	1.01	7-5	1.02
5-6	0.99	6-6	1.00
4-7	0.97	5-7	0.98
3-8	0.95	4-8	0.96
2-9	0.93	3-9	0.94
1-10	0.91	2-10	0.92
0-11	0.89	1-11	0.90
		0-12	0.88

If a team should happen to play thirteen or fourteen games, the same process is used. If a team has a 9–4 record, for example, the initial weight would be 1.05, since there were five more wins than losses. Counting all wins over Bowl Subdivision teams does not directly benefit the team with the 9–4 record, though. It only helps determine the initial weight of that team.

The Final Weight

After the IW has been established, adjustments are made to develop the final weight (FW). As with the initial weight, the final weight can be determined at any time during the season and only considers the games played up to that point. This enables standings to be computed after games each week. As pointed out in the criteria, the adjustments are made only for wins against winning teams and losses to losing teams. Defeating a winning team is considered a sign of strength, and losing to a losing team is considered a sign of weakness. For example, suppose a team with a 10–2 record has defeated teams with records of 11–1, 7–5, 9–3, 8–4 and six losing teams. Suppose both losses were to winning teams. Adjustments to the IW are calculated thus:

> 1.08 (IW or initial weight of team with a 10-2 record)
> + 0.10 (for win over 11-1 team, ten more wins than losses)
> + 0.02 (for win over 7-5 team, two more wins than losses)
> + 0.06 (for win over 9-3 team, six more wins than losses)
> + 0.04 (for win over 8-4 team, four more wins than losses)
> 1.30 = final weight for this team

Since defeating a losing team and losing to a winning team do not affect the final weight, the only adjustments to the initial weight for the team in this example are the four that are illustrated above.

Another example may better illustrate how the initial weight of a team decreases by losing to a losing team. Suppose a team with a 5–6 record loses to three winning teams, a team with a 4–7 record, a team with a 3–8 record, and a team that is not in the Bowl Subdivision, for a total of six losses. Also, suppose four of the wins were over losing teams and the other win was over a team with a 6–5 record. Adjustments to the IW are thus:

> 0.99 (IW of team with a 5–6 record)
> − 0.03 (for loss to 4–7 team, three more losses than wins)
> − 0.05 (for loss to 3–8 team, five more losses than wins)
> − 0.10 (all losses to non-Bowl Subdivision teams are -0.10)
> + 0.01 (for win over 6–5 team, one more win than losses)
> 0.82 = final weight for this team

As described in the criteria, there are no adjustments for the wins over the losing teams or the losses to the winning teams.

Determining Standings: Weighted Wins

The weighted wins for a given team is simply the sum of the final weights of the opponents it defeated. For example, if a team defeats an opponent with a final weight of 1.23, the winning team receives a weighted win of 1.23. To defeat a team with an FW of 0.97, the winning team receives a weighted win of 0.97.

Weighted Losses

To determine the weighted loss, two numerical values are needed. The value of the loss is the final weight of the winning team minus the initial weight of the losing team (FW – IW). Teams that lose to quality opponents are not penalized as severely as those losing to teams with losing records. For example, say, a team with a 9-3 record (IW = 1.06) loses to a team with an FW of 1.17. The weighted loss in this case is 0.11, since 1.17 – 1.06 = 0.11. The value 0.11 is the weighted loss, and this value is added to the weighted wins total. On the other hand, suppose that same 9-3 team loses to a team with an FW of 0.97. In this example, the weighted loss would be -0.09, since 0.97 – 1.06 = -0.09. The weighted wins total would decrease by 0.09 since a negative value was obtained. After a short discussion about weighted losses, we will then examine two team's complete season schedules to fully illustrate the weighted wins process.

Some Notes about Weighted Losses

The concept of weighted loss corresponds to the concept of weighted wins. The value of the win or loss is an attempt to illustrate the strength differences of the teams involved. To further demonstrate, let's take a look at two examples from 2019.

In that season, Penn State, which had an IW of 1.07, lost to Ohio State, which had an FW of 1.58. Penn State's weighted loss is the difference between Ohio State's FW and Penn State's IW, or 1.58 − 1.07 = 0.51. Note that Penn State's IW of 1.07 came from their having a 10–2 record with one game against a non-Bowl Subdivision team, thus, seven more wins than losses against Bowl Subdivision teams. Even though it was a loss, the 0.51 value still contributed to Penn State's entry in the total win column for that Ohio State game.

Also, in 2019, an 8–4 Oklahoma State team lost to 4–8 Texas Tech. Each team had played a non-Bowl Subdivision team; therefore, Oklahoma State had an IW of 1.03 since it had three more wins than losses against Bowl Subdivision teams. Texas Tech had also played a non-Bowl Subdivision team, so its IW was 0.95 since it had five more losses than wins. Texas Tech, however, had lost to three losing teams to end up with an FW of 0.83. So applying the same methodology, we take the winning team's FW and subtract the losing team's IW, or 0.83 − 1.03 = -0.20. Oklahoma State's loss would be considered a "bad loss" and would have a negative effect on its total win value. To further view this example, just visit the Weighted Wins website, view the 2019 standings, and click on Oklahoma State.

From these two examples, you can see how much difference there is between losing to a strong team and losing to a weak team. These differences are one reason that makes weighted wins truly effective.

Full Season Weighted Wins Examples

Let's take a look at the 2005 Boise State season. Oregon State had one win over a non-Bowl Subdivision opponent, so it had two more losses than wins against Bowl Subdivision teams (hence the -0.020 FW adjustment). When calculating the weighted wins and weighted losses for Boise State, you first count the three losses and then add the seven best wins, for a total of ten games. As described in the WW criteria, the two weakest wins (Idaho and non-Bowl

Subdivision) are dropped. Boise State ends up with a final weighted wins value of 6.70.

Boise State
(2005 Results)

Record: 9-3

Initial Weight: 1.05

Adjustments to Initial Weight: 0.070

Final Weight: 1.12

Weighted Wins: 6.70

Opponent	Result	FW Adj	Opp FW	Value Added
Georgia (10-2)	L	0.000	1.260	0.210
Oregon State (5-6)	L	-0.020	0.980	-0.070
Bowling Green (6-5)	W	0.010	1.040	1.040
Hawaii (6-7)	W	0.000	0.980	0.980
Non-Bowl Subdivision	W	0.000	0.000	Drop
San Jose State (3-8)	W	0.000	0.770	0.770
Utah State (3-8)	W	0.000	0.870	0.870
Nevada (8-3)	W	0.050	1.070	1.070
New Mexico State (1-12)	W	0.000	0.700	0.700
Fresno State (8-4)	L	0.000	1.120	0.070
Idaho (2-9)	W	0.000	0.680	Drop
Louisiana Tech (7-4)	W	0.030	1.060	1.060
Total:		0.070		6.700

Let's consider another example that will further illustrate the weighted wins system. In this case, we will examine Oklahoma's 2015 season. You can see that Oklahoma went 11–1, which gives an initial weight of 1.10. Since eleven of the twelve games must be counted, the loss versus Texas is automatically reflected in the weighted wins. Losing to a losing team will actually reflect a negative score in the overall weighted wins. The lowest-valued win, Kansas with a value of

0.630, is then dropped from the overall weighted wins score. When summing up the negative value from the Texas loss and the top 10 wins, Oklahoma ended up with a weighted wins value of 10.520. The Texas defeat, what could be called a "bad loss" since it was to a team with a losing record, ultimately cost it a top 4 position in the final weighted wins standings. Note: we switched from counting ten games to eleven games when most schools began playing twelve-game schedules.

Oklahoma
(2015 Results)

Record: 11-1   Initial Weight: 1.10
Adjustments to Initial Weight: 0.230   Final Weight: 1.33
Weighted Wins: 10.520

Opponent	Result	FW Adj	Opp FW	Value Added
Akron (7-5)	W	0.010	1.010	1.010
Tennessee (8-4)	W	0.030	1.150	1.150
Tulsa (6-6)	W	0.000	0.980	0.980
West Virginia (7-5)	W	0.010	1.040	1.040
Texas (5-7)	L	-0.020	1.060	-0.040
Kansas State (6-6)	W	0.000	1.010	1.010
Texas Tech (7-5)	W	0.010	1.020	1.020
Kansas (0-12)	W	0.000	0.630	Drop
Iowa State (3-9)	W	0.000	0.920	0.920
Baylor (9-3)	W	0.050	1.120	1.120
Texas Christian (10-2)	W	0.070	1.140	1.140
Oklahoma State (10-2)	W	0.070	1.170	1.170
	Total	0.230		10.520

CHAPTER 4

COMPARING SYSTEMS

No, nobody does. Each year it looks like there are different variables that are going to factor in because there are different people sitting in the room. That's going to happen. One person is going to have a bias toward one thing. It's natural. Somebody will have a bias toward another, and some people are going to feel like this is a more important metric.

—James Franklin,
Penn State football coach,
when asked if he understood the
current CFP ranking system

Since Division I Bowl Subdivision college football is the only major sport that doesn't have a well-defined system for selecting playoff teams, efforts to develop a suitable system are challenging. The current method, using a selection committee to decide the playoff teams, is not well received by the general fan population. There is a perception that the media, conference protectionism, and name recognition have too much influence on the process. In this chapter, we will compare our weighted wins model to the rankings from the poll-based pre-BCS era, the BCS era, and the CFP committee era.

Pre BCS

Before the introduction of the BCS, there weren't very many inter-conference games, and conferences didn't have championship tournaments. In fact, the conferences didn't necessarily play a full, round-robin schedule. Additionally, most bowl matchups were tied to specific conferences. For example, the Rose Bowl always matched a Big Ten team against a Pac-10 team—usually the conference champions. Unless both champions had strong seasons, the bowl game results didn't really help that much in determining the final standings.

Nevertheless, prior to the bowl games, ten out of seventeen years, weighted wins had the eventual national champion ranked at the top of the standings. In every year except one, the team that eventually was declared national champion finished in the top 4. That lone exception occurred in 1989. Going into the bowl games, the University of Miami was fifth in the weighted wins standings and won its bowl game. At the same time, the teams ranked first and third both lost their bowl games, while Miami had defeated the second-place team during the regular season. Now that teams are competing in conference championships and are playing more nonconference games, the weighted wins model yields even stronger results, with greater separation in the standings.

The BCS Era

A complete analysis of the BCS era is included in chapter 5. As that analysis shows, during eleven of the sixteen years of the BCS, the weighted wins model had the eventual national champion number 1 in its standings before the championship game was played. Weighted wins fared better than either the polls or the computer models utilized by the BCS formula. In twelve of the sixteen years, weighted wins had both teams in the playoffs. In the other four years, the third-ranked team won the national championship three times, and the fourth-ranked team won the championship in the remaining year. In every year of the BCS, given a four-team playoff, the eventual national champion was included among the top 4 in the weighted wins standings.

As is detailed in chapter 5, when comparing the weighted wins model to the various polls and computer models, the weighted wins model proves to be better at identifying the best teams.

CFP Committee

In all seven years of the CFP committee's selections, the weighted wins model and the CPF committee agreed on at least three of the four playoff teams. In one year, both models agreed on the same four teams. In every instance but one, where differences occurred, a Group of Five team slipped into the playoff mix in regard to the weighted wins standings. Beginning with the 2014 and 2015 seasons, here is a more detailed analysis of the comparisons:

2014

CFP Committee	Weighted Wins
1. Alabama	1. Florida State
2. Oregon	2. Alabama
3. Florida State	3. Oregon
4. Ohio State	4. Ohio State

2015

CFP Committee	Weighted Wins
1. Clemson	1. Clemson
2. Alabama	2. Alabama
3. Michigan State	3. Michigan State
4. Oklahoma	4. Ohio State
5. NA	5. Oklahoma

In 2015, the difference between Ohio State and Oklahoma was very small in the weighted wins column. However, weighted wins counts all games throughout the season and playoffs identically. All wins and losses receive what are called weighted wins and weighted losses. Oklahoma had lost to a losing team that had a negative weighted loss. Since Ohio State lost to a team with an 11-1 record, coincidentally, in the conference playoff, the weighted wins treated that loss more favorably.

2016

CFP Committee	Weighted Wins
1. Alabama	1. Alabama
2. Clemson	2. Ohio State
3. Ohio State	3. Clemson
4. Washington	4. Western Michigan

The 2016 season was the first year since 2009 in which a Group of Five conference member reached the top 4 in weighted wins. Although Western Michigan lost its bowl game by one score to a top-rated team, Washington lost by three scores in its CFP game. Who is to say which team was more deserving? One thing is certain: a Group of Five member is playing against greater odds of making the playoff, partly because of name recognition.

2017

CFP Committee	Weighted Wins
1. Clemson	1. Clemson
2. Oklahoma	2. Central Florida
3. Georgia	3. Georgia
4. Alabama	4. Oklahoma
5. Wisconsin	5. Wisconsin
6. Central Florida	6. Alabama

In the 2017 season, since weighted wins doesn't have name recognition but applies the criteria evenly to all teams, the apparent conference protectionism was on full display. Alabama did not win its division of the SEC, having lost to Auburn. However, Alabama was selected over Wisconsin, who lost its conference championship game by less than one score. It was Wisconsin's only loss of the season. In turn, Auburn lost to Georgia in the SEC conference championship game. As a side note, Central Florida then defeated Auburn in its bowl game.

Several questions arise from this scenario. How does a Group of Five team qualify for the CFP championship playoff? Is it better to not have to put yourself at risk in one more high-profile game if you have name recognition? Wisconsin certainly would have been in the playoffs had it opted out of the Big Ten championship game. Of course, it would never have done so.

For the first time in forty years, a team as low as sixth in weighted wins won the national championship. It was also the first time in forty years that a Group of Five team reached as high as second in weighted wins. The selection committee seemed to be vindicated by the fact that Alabama won the national championship. However, looking at it another way, one may conclude that the other teams in discussion were denied the opportunity to compete for the championship. Opportunity comes before success.

Kirk Herbstreit, an analyst for ESPN's *College GameDay* addressed this issue at that time. "I think it's very concerning to all the other teams that aren't the blue bloods or those teams with tradition. And we've got to revisit that. We've got to tweak it. Instead of putting our heads in the sand [saying], 'Well, those other teams got to get better,' well, that's not necessarily the case. I think the teams need an opportunity," said Herbstreit.

2018

CFP Committee	Weighted Wins
1. Alabama	1. Clemson
2. Clemson	2. Alabama
3. Notre Dame	3. Notre Dame
4. Oklahoma	4. Central Florida
5. Georgia	5. Ohio State
6. Ohio State	6. Oklahoma

In 2018, although Central Florida had a twenty-five-game winning streak, the CFP committee still overlooked it for the playoffs. While losing by only one score to a SEC team in the Fiesta Bowl in a high-scoring game, it again displayed the ability to be a worthy opponent.

In his article "UCF Didn't Lose a Game—but the Knights Lost to College Football's Cartel," which appeared in the South Carolina University publication *The Ringer*, Michael Baumann wrote, "After a second consecutive undefeated season failed to earn Central Florida a playoff spot, it's clear that the sport's power structure will never let the Knights—or the best Group of Five team of any season—have a shot at the national title game." This article best describes the sentiment of many true college football fans. Is the current system truly a Division I championship, or is it merely a Power Five championship?

2019

CFP Committee	Weighted Wins
1. LSU	1. Ohio State
2. Ohio State	2. LSU
3. Clemson	3. Clemson
4. Oklahoma	4. Memphis

In 2019, it was a 12-1 Memphis team that was on the outside looking in. Does anyone think that Memphis would have lost in a playoff game by more than 63–28? The final score of the first-round semifinal game was LSU, 63; Oklahoma, 28.

2020

CFP Committee	Weighted Wins
1. Alabama	1. Alabama
2. Clemson	2. Coastal Carolina
3. Ohio State	3. Notre Dame
4. Notre Dame	4. Clemson

The 2020 season was anything but normal. COVID-19 cancellations and postponements caused many teams and conferences to play abbreviated schedules. As a result, some teams played almost a full schedule, some a half-schedule, and some barely a quarter of their regular season schedule. There were no interconference games, and as a result, the differences in weights were not as pronounced as in a normal season.

In the first six years of the current CFP system, the highest average weighted wins score was over 1.44, while the lowest average score was 0.62. The highest weighted win in 2020 was 1.32, and the lowest was 0.72. These differences led to a huge difference in the season's total weighted wins. Even with these differences, weighted wins had identified three of the four teams in the playoffs. Ohio State was the only exception since it only played half of its schedule and didn't show up on the radar. Which schools would have been in the playoffs had every team played a full schedule is anyone's guess.

CHAPTER 5

EVALUATING WEIGHTED WINS

There are two things every man in America thinks he can do: work a grill and coach football.

—Greg Schiano,
Rutgers football coach

In this chapter, we present an analysis of historical data to show how the weighted wins model compares to the polls and other ranking systems that have been used to determine playoff qualifiers and eventual national champions.

In this first table, we looked at the AP poll, the UPI coaches poll, and weighted wins, using results from the 1981 through 1997 seasons—the seventeen years immediately preceding the introduction of the Bowl Championship Series. These rankings and standings are all based on data from the end of the season, before any bowl games had been played. The table shows that weighted wins was basically on the same page as the two polls.

Comparison of Ranking Systems for pre-BCS Era
Seventeen-Year Period from 1981 to 1997

Year	Rank	AP Poll	UPI/Coaches Poll	Weighted Wins	
1981	(1)	Clemson	Clemson	Clemson	9.74
	(2)	Georgia	Georgia	Georgia	8.85
1982	(1)	Georgia	Georgia	Georgia	10.57
	(2)	Penn State	Penn State	Penn State	9.87
1983	(1)	Nebraska	Nebraska	Texas	10.13
	(2)	Texas	Texas	Auburn	10.10
	(3)	Auburn	Auburn	Nebraska	10.06
1984	(1)	Brigham Young	Brigham Young	Brigham Young	9.58
	(2)	Oklahoma	Oklahoma	Florida	9.23
	(3)	Florida	Washington	Washington	9.12
1985	(1)	Penn State	Penn State	Penn State	9.96
	(2)	Miami Fla.	Oklahoma	Miami Fla.	9.42
	(3)	Oklahoma	Iowa	Florida	9.30
1986	(1)	Miami Fla.	Miami Fla.	Penn State	10.23
	(2)	Penn State	Penn State	Miami Fla.	10.21
1987	(1)	Oklahoma	Oklahoma	Miami Fla.	10.39
	(2)	Miami Fla.	Miami Fla.	Oklahoma	9.76
1988	(1)	Notre Dame	Notre Dame	Notre Dame	10.82
	(2)	Miami Fla.	Miami Fla.	Miami Fla.	10.28
1989	(1)	Colorado	Colorado	Colorado	10.52
	(2)	Miami Fla.	Miami Fla.	Notre Dame	10.06
1990	(1)	Colorado	Colorado	Georgia Tech	9.63
	(2)	Georgia Tech	Georgia Tech	Texas	9.59
	(3)	Texas	Texas	Colorado	9.54

1991	(1)	Miami Fla.	Washington	Miami Fla.	10.69
	(2)	Washington	Miami Fla.	Washington	10.22
1992	(1)	Miami Fla.	Miami Fla.	Alabama	10.35
	(2)	Alabama	Alabama	Miami Fla.	10.20
1993	(1)	Florida State	Nebraska	West Virginia	10.23
	(2)	Nebraska	West Virginia	Nebraska	10.18
	(3)	West Virginia	Florida State	Auburn	10.05
1994	(1)	Nebraska	Nebraska	Penn State	10.48
	(2)	Penn State	Penn State	Nebraska	10.28
1995	(1)	Nebraska	Nebraska	Florida	10.52
	(2)	Florida	Florida	Nebraska	10.41
1996	(1)	Florida State	Florida State	Florida State	10.67
	(2)	Arizona State	Arizona State	Arizona State	10.31
1997	(1)	Michigan	Michigan	Michigan	10.57
	(2)	Nebraska	Nebraska	Nebraska	10.32

This second table examines the weighted wins results from the 1998 through 2013 seasons—the sixteen years of the Bowl Championship Series (BCS) era. Once again, the data used to determine the weighted wins scores does not include bowl game results. Rather than including direct comparisons with poll results, the table lists the top 8 weighted wins teams, with the eventual national champion displayed in italics, and the AP poll's top-ranked team underlined. Again, it is easy to see visually that weighted wins is in alignment with the AP poll.

Summary of Weighted Wins Standings
between 1998 and 2013

2013	2012	2011	2010
1. *Florida State*	1. Notre Dame	1. LSU	1. *Auburn*
2. Auburn	2. Florida	2. Oklahoma State	2. Oregon
3. Michigan State	3. *Alabama*	3. *Alabama*	3. TCU
4. Ohio State	4. Oregon	4. Stanford	4. Oklahoma
5. Alabama	5. Kansas State	5. Houston	5. Ohio State
6. Stanford	6. Stanford	6. Kansas State	6. Michigan State
7. Baylor	7. LSU	7. Boise State	7. Stanford
8. Missouri	8. Oklahoma	8. Virginia Tech	8. Missouri
2009	2008	2007	2006
1. *Alabama*	1. Oklahoma	1. Missouri	1. *Florida*
2. Texas	2. Texas	2. Ohio State	2. Ohio State
3. Cincinnati	3. Utah	3. *LSU*	3. Louisville
4. Florida	4. *Florida*	4. Virginia Tech	4. Boise State
5. Boise State	5. Boise State	5. Georgia	5. Michigan
6. TCU	6. USC	6. Kansas	6. USC
7. Oregon	7. Penn State	7. Oklahoma	7. LSU
8. Georgia Tech	8. Alabama	8. West Virginia	8. Auburn
2005	2004	2003	2002
1. *Texas*	1. *USC*	1. Oklahoma	1. *Ohio State*
2. USC	2. Oklahoma	2. *LSU*	2. Miami Fla.
3. Penn State	3. Auburn	3. USC	3. Georgia
4. Virginia Tech	4. Utah	4. Ohio State	4. USC
5. Ohio State	5. Texas	5. Miami Fla.	5. Oklahoma
6. Miami Fla.	6. Boise State	6. Texas	6. Iowa
7. Georgia	7. California	7. Michigan	7. Texas
8. TCU	8. Virginia Tech	8. Florida State	8. Notre Dame

2001	2000	1999	1998
1. *Miami Fla.*	1. *Oklahoma*	1. *Florida State*	1. *Tennessee*
2. Nebraska	2. Florida State	2. Virginia Tech	2. Florida State
3. Oregon	3. Washington	3. Nebraska	3. UCLA
4. Tennessee	4. Miami Fla.	4. Marshall	4. Kansas State
5. Illinois	5. Virginia Tech	5. Kansas State	5. Ohio State
6. Colorado	6. Oregon State	6. Alabama	6. Tulane
7. Florida	7. Florida	7. Tennessee	7. Arizona
8. Maryland	8. Nebraska	8. Michigan	8. Texas A&M

Notes: Weighted wins top 8 standings are prior to any bowl matchups. Underlined teams are the number 1 ranked AP team heading into the bowl season. Italics denotes the eventual national champion after the bowl games.

In this third table, we compared the weighted wins model to the other components that were used in the BCS formula from 1998 to 2013. More specifically, we first looked at how often each of these components had both the number 1 and number 2 teams in the BCS championship game. As you can see from the table, weighted wins compared favorably, getting the numbers 1 and 2 teams correct 75 percent (twelve of sixteen) of the time. Since some of these systems were not used in the BCS for all sixteen years, we sorted the success rate by the percentage of time that both of the top 2 teams were identified.

Comparison of BCS Formula Components with Weighted Wins between 1998 and 2013

BCS Component That Had Both Numbers 1 and 2 Teams in the Championship Game

Ranking System	Years	Both Top 2	Percent
Harris Poll and AP	16	13	81
Coaches Poll	16	13	81
Billingsley	15	12	80
Weighted Wins*	16	12	75
Colley Matrix	13	9	69
Anderson & Hester	16	10	63
Wolfe	13	8	62
Massey	15	9	60
Sagarin	16	9	56

*Weighted wins was not a component of the BCS formula.

Although weighted wins was designed to be an evaluative tool and not intended to be predictive, we thought it would be interesting to see how each of these ranking systems fared in having the eventual national champion rated number 1 prior to the bowl game match-ups. As you can see from our fourth table, weighted wins actually had the highest success rate, correctly ranking the eventual national champion number 1, going into the bowl season, eleven out of six-teen times, for a rate of 69 percent. This was higher than all the computer systems, media poll, and coaches poll.

Had National Champion Rated Number 1 before the National Championship Game

Ranking System	Years	Rated No. 1	Percent
Weighted Wins*	16	11	69
Massey	15	7	47
Colley	13	6	46
Harris Poll and AP	16	7	44
Billingsly	15	6	40
Anderson & Hester	16	6	38
Sagarin	16	6	38
Wolfe	13	4	31
Coaches Poll	16	5	31

*Weighted wins was not a component of the BCS formula.

Finally, we wanted to take a look at how weighted wins compared to the College Football Playoff (CFP) since its inception in 2014 through 2020. In this fifth table, we compared the list of teams chosen by the College Football Playoff selection committee, with the top 6 teams in the weighted wins model going into the bowl season. Again, we use italics to highlight the eventual national champion.

Comparison of CFP Selection Committee and Weighted Wins 2014–2020

Selection Committee's Picks	Weighted Wins Standings
2020	
1. *Alabama*	1. *Alabama*
2. Clemson	2. Coastal Carolina
3. Ohio State	3. Notre Dame
4. Notre Dame	4. Clemson
5. Texas A&M	5. Brigham Young
6. Oklahoma	6. Louisiana-Lafayette
2019	
1. *Louisiana State*	1. Ohio State
2. Ohio State	2. *Louisiana State*
3. Clemson	3. Clemson
4. Oklahoma	4. Memphis
5. Georgia	5. Oklahoma
6. Oregon	6. Boise State
2018	
1. Alabama	1. *Clemson*
2. *Clemson*	2. Alabama
3. Notre Dame	3. Notre Dame
4. Oklahoma	4. Ohio State
5. Georgia	5. Oklahoma
6. Ohio State	6. Georgia

RAY D. THEIS AND MARK G. TERWILLIGER

2017

1. Clemson	1. Clemson
2. Oklahoma	2. Central Florida
3. Georgia	3. Georgia
4. *Alabama*	4. Oklahoma
5. Wisconsin (6)	5. Wisconsin
6. Central Florida (12)	6. *Alabama*

2016

1. Alabama	1. Alabama
2. *Clemson*	2. Ohio State
3. Ohio State	3. *Clemson*
4. Washington	4. Western Michigan
5. NA	6. Washington

2015

1. Clemson	1. Clemson
2. *Alabama*	2. *Alabama*
3. Michigan State	3. Michigan State
4. Oklahoma	4. Ohio State
5. NA	5. Oklahoma

2014

1. Alabama	1. Florida State
2. Oregon	2. Alabama
3. Florida State	3. Oregon
4. *Ohio State*	4. *Ohio State*

The 2017 season was the first time in forty years where the eventual national champion was ranked outside of the top 4 by the weighted wins model. In that season, Auburn had defeated Alabama in the regular season but ended up losing its bowl game to Central Florida. Because of the regular season loss, Alabama had fallen to number 6 in the weighted wins model but eventually ended up winning the national championship.

In this final table, we compared the weighted wins model with the various BCS formula components for the two seasons following the abandonment of the formula-based selection system. We examined the top 5 teams for the eight BCS formula components to see how each measured up with the CFP selection committee's top 5 and the weighted win standings' top 5. From these tables, you can compare how the coaches poll, media poll, computer systems, and weighted wins do as far as choosing the same four teams that played in the CFP semifinal games. In these tables, we use italics to highlight the four playoff teams.

Post-BCS Football Ranking Comparisons of BCS Formula Components and Weighted Wins, 2014 and 2015, with Selection Committee's Final Choices

	2014 Sel Com	AP	Coaches	A&H	Bil	Col	Mas	Sag	Wol	WW
(1)	*Ala*	*Ala*	*Ala*	*FSU*	*FSU*	*FSU*	*Ala*	*Ala*	*FSU*	*FSU*
(2)	*Ore*	*FSU*	*FSU*	*Ore*	*Ala*	*Ala*	*Ore*	*Ore*	*Ala*	*Ala*
(3)	*FSU*	*Ore*	*Ore*	*Ala*	*Ore*	*OSU*	TCU	TCU	*Ore*	*Ore*
(4)	*OSU*	Bay	*OSU*	*OSU*	*OSU*	*Ore*	*FSU*	*OSU*	*OSU*	*OSU*
(5)	Bay	*OSU*	Bay	TCU	TCU	TCU	*OSU*	*FSU**	TCU	TCU

*FSU made the four-team playoff but was only ranked seventh by Sagarin.

	2015 Sel Com	AP	Coaches	A&H	Bil	Col	Mas	Sag	Wol	WW
(1)	*Clem*	*Clem*	*Clem*	*Clem*	*Clem*	Ala	Ala	Ala	*Clem*	*Clem*
(2)	*Ala*	*Ala*	*Ala*	*MSU*	*Ala*	*MSU*	Okl	Okl	*MSU*	*Ala*
(3)	*MSU*	*MSU*	Okl	*Ala*	*MSU*	Clem	Clem	Clem	Ala	*MSU*
(4)	*Okl*	*Okl*	MSU	*Okl*	*Okl*	*Okl*	OSU	OSU	Iowa	OSU
(5)	Iowa	Sta	OSU	Iowa	OSU	OSU	*MSU*	*MSU*	Okl	Okl

*MSU made the four-team playoff but was only ranked ninth by Sagarin.

Legend for both tables: Harris poll and AP, *AP*; coaches poll, *coaches*; Anderson & Hester, *A&H*; Billingsley, *Bil*; Colley Matrix, *Col*; Massey, *Mas*; Sagarin, *Sag*; Wol, *Wolfe*; and weighted wins, *WW*.

Conclusions

As illustrated, weighted wins had more success in identifying the eventual national champion than any component of the BCS formula or even the BCS formula itself. Weighted Wins had 69 percent accuracy, while none of the BCS components, polls or computers, had even 50 percent accuracy in identifying the national champion before the game itself.

The weighted wins system has a built-in strength-of-schedule factor that becomes apparent as the season progresses. The well-defined objective nature of weighted wins produces consistent and accurate results on a year-to-year basis.

CHAPTER 6

WHERE DO WE GO FROM HERE?

I never graduated from Iowa, but I was only there for two terms—Truman's and Eisenhower's.

—Alex Karras,
former University of Iowa football player

We have some more controversies to discuss. We also need to talk about where we go from here. In this chapter, we will try to tie it all together and make a final convincing argument on why we believe weighted wins should strongly be considered to choose the finalists for the college football playoffs.

The Big Three

What effect does the closed-door policy (Alabama, Clemson, and Ohio State) have on college football in general and recruiting in particular? In the table below, we show the number of times various conferences have been represented in the College Football Playoffs:

Conference	Playoff Appearance	Teams Involved
ACC	8	Clemson, 6; Florida State, 1; and Notre Dame,* 1
SEC	8	Alabama, 6; Georgia, 1; and LSU, 1
Big Ten	5	Ohio State, 4, and Michigan State, 1
Big 12	4	Oklahoma, 4
Pac-12	2	Oregon, 1, and Washington, 1
Independents	2	Notre Dame, 2 (once as member of ACC)

A recent ESPN commentator said that he could predict three of the four teams that would be in the playoffs next year, and not only that, he could also predict three of the four teams that would be in the playoffs in 2023 (Alabama, Clemson, and Ohio State). Does this create a recruiting magnet for those teams?

The preceding table and narrative clearly denote the closed-door policy of the CFP selection committee. As the data illustrates, only 11 of 130 Division I Bowl Subdivision teams have ever been selected for the playoffs.

Final Thoughts

In the review of the different eras of college football, much was revealed about the biases, inconsistencies, and lack of transparency in the different systems. In our forty-year study, the Associated Press (AP) preseason favorite only won the national championship three times. Although preseason polls create great fan interest and controversy, they also build a degree of unfairness into the system for many of the teams. The carryover of team value from one year to the next is very difficult to overlook. In twelve of forty years, the AP poll selected the previous year's national champion as the preseason favorite. Despite their fan appeal and ability to generate fan interest, the preseason polls have been shown to have very little predictive value. To quote Yogi Berra, "It's tough to make predictions, especially about the future." In this case, we are predicting every game in the season.

In the Bowl Championship Series (BCS) era, computer-based models were added to the process in an effort to create a fairer system for selecting participants for the two-team playoff. Ironically, though, some of the computer models carried over data from the previous year to create their early season rankings. Again, information from the previous year was conflated with the current year to bias the rankings. How much carryover is there in Major League Baseball, the NBA, or the NFL from one year to the next? In these sports, every team starts the new season with no wins and no losses, and standings are created game by game—scores be damned.

When the BCS formula was replaced by the College Football Playoff committee, the selection committee was charged with choosing the best teams to compete in a four-team playoff. The thirteen-member blue ribbon committee is composed of high-profile administrators, former coaches, and former players. This committee was intended to do what two polls, based on approximately one hundred voters, and five computer models couldn't manage—identify the four best college football teams in the country. During the BCS era, computer models that utilized the margin of victory were either dropped from the BCS formula or forced to eliminate that factor. In the CFP era, the "eye test" and "style points" were promoted by the media, and the phrases became key talking points. This led to terms such as *bad losses* and *signature wins*, which had the opposite effect of removing the margin of victory during the BCS era. Teams were encouraged to throw out sportsmanship and run up the scores in order to gain recognition. The effect of the current CFP system is creating superpowers within the Power Five conferences. Highly sought-after athletes are more easily recruited to teams with a high likelihood of participating in the national playoffs.

In five of the seven years of the CFP, a Group of Five team made the top 4 in weighted wins. In order to open the door to all Bowl Subdivision football teams, why not develop some schematic that would enable a Group of Five team to be included? This does not mean expanding the playoffs to eight teams. If the highest-ranked Group of Five team has not played at least one winning Power Five team, then that team would need to defeat the number 5 team in the weighted wins standings. This would require only one extra game, with a well-defined path to the playoffs. It provides the transparency, consistency, objectivity, and validity needed in an acceptable system. All teams start the season with no wins and no losses, with no carry-over influence from the previous year.

Teams work their way to the top of the standings through their weekly performance. This is much like what happens in MLB, the NBA, and the NFL. There is a completely objective method for defining the path to the national playoffs for all Bowl Subdivision teams. The weighted wins formula does not recognize the names of the teams or the conferences. The weighted wins system applies the same criteria to all teams. Our forty-year study shows that the system coincides very closely with actual outcomes, although with two major exceptions. There are no political influences, and every Bowl Subdivision team is treated identically. Weighted wins does away with the eye test and style points, as margin of victory is not important. The concepts of "bad loss" and "signature win" are also diminished, since the weighted win or weighted loss of each game is evaluated directly. If two 11–0 teams play, the winner's signature win will automatically be reflected in its weighted wins score, while a loss to a team with a losing record is similarly reflected. Refer to the Oklahoma schedule in chapter 3 for a perfect example.

Probably the most egregious miss in the seven years of the CFP was the selection committee dismissing Central Florida from consideration to play in the 2017 playoffs. The full breakdown of this snub is discussed in chapter 4.

The fallacy of the CFP committee is its attempt to identify the four "best" teams in college football. When the criteria are so nebulous, subjective, and constantly changing, consistency is virtually impossible. A better approach would be to qualify the four teams on the basis of their complete résumés. Using a team's full résumé makes every game during the season important.

To recap our recommendation, the weighted wins model could be used to replace the CFP. At the end of the season, the top of the weighted wins standings reflects the four best résumés in college football. If one of those is a Group of Five team and that team has not defeated a Power Five team with a winning record, then a special play-in game would be scheduled against the Power Five team with the next highest standing.

An eight-team playoff is not necessary. In the history of college football, only one team with two losses has won the national championship. To real college football fans, this is a traditional value to uphold. College basketball effectively has a six-game season, the March Madness tournament. College football doesn't need a three-game season. Every game in the season is important, as it is résumé-building.

In summary, these are the main strengths of the weighted wins system:

1. Complete transparency.
2. Easy to understand; simple mathematics is utilized.
3. Consistent from year to year with every season, starting with zero wins and zero losses. No carryover from previous year.
4. Completely objective; does not recognize name of team.
5. Fairness of system, as all teams from all conferences have a path to the playoffs.
6. Validity confirmed by high correlation with the polls.

CHAPTER 7

THE WEIGHTED WINS WEBSITE

No. No. The purest evidence that you can't trust them to get it right is the fact we weren't in the top 8 last year. In the end you look at the votes, and it pretty well reflected where the members of the committee were from.

—Mike Leach,
Washington State football coach,
when asked if he trusted the
CFP selection committee

Like many great ideas, one of the book's authors, Ray, came up with the idea for the weighted wins system back in the late eighties as debates occurred over morning coffees with friend Ed Kimminau. With about a thousand games per season, though, Ray needed a way to automate the weighted wins model so he could evaluate its performance over many years. In 2001, Ray, Ed, and one of Ray's former college buddies, Gary Thesing, met up with Mark, the other book author, to discuss weighted wins.

A complete standings view from the original Weighted Wins software.

When Ray explained the weighted wins system, Gary and Mark both agreed that he was onto something. At that time in college football, many computer ranking systems were being used. The formulas were complex and sometimes not shared. This weighted wins system to evaluate teams was very straightforward and easy to understand. Teams were not rewarded for running up the score against weak opponents; the system rewards you for beating good teams and penalizes you for losing to bad teams.

After this first meeting in 2001, it was obvious that a computer program would need to be developed to implement the weighted wins system. The first version was written by Mark using Delphi, an object-oriented version of the Pascal programming language. It provided a graphical user interface that allowed the user, mainly Ray, to enter results of games and view the standings for any particular year. You can see the Standings View of this original Windows-based software on the previous page. The Team View of Georgia's 2004 season is shown below:

Individual Team Results			— □ ×	

Georgia Season Results
Record: 9-2   Initial Weight: 1.060
Adjustments to Initial Weight: 0.120   Final Weight: 1.180
Weighted Wins 8.260

Opponent	Result	FW Adj	Opp FW	Value Added
Georgia Tech (6-5)	W	0.000	1.030	1.030
Non-Division I-A (6-50)	W	0.000	0.000	DROP
South Carolina (6-5)	W	0.010	1.000	1.000
Marshall (6-5)	W	0.010	1.040	1.040
Louisiana State (9-2)	W	0.070	1.130	1.130
Tennessee (9-3)	L	0.000	1.160	0.100
Vanderbilt (2-9)	W	0.000	0.790	0.790
Arkansas (5-6)	W	0.000	0.990	0.990
Florida (7-4)	W	0.030	1.040	1.040
Kentucky (2-9)	W	0.000	0.840	0.840
Auburn (12-0)	L	0.000	1.360	0.300
	Total:	0.120		8.260

🏛 Close			Print Team Results	

A season schedule view from the original Weighted Wins software.

This Windows-based software worked great for about ten years, until the authors wanted to share the weighted wins system for others to view and provide feedback. It was obvious a web-based implementation was required, so a complete overhaul was necessary. The current web-based system was initially developed in 2004 and provides the same basic features as the Windows version.

Weighted Wins

NCAA Division I Football Standings

Menu

WW Home

How Weights are Determined

How Standings are Determined

WW Criteria

WW Standings

About WW

Administration

Other Links

WW vs. Selection Committee

BCS Standings: 1998-2012

16-year WW summary

WW vs. BCS components

Weighted Wins

The basic premise of "Weighted Wins" is one the average fan would readily accept. All wins are not equal. Defeating a highly successful team, one with a winning record, is more difficult than defeating an unsuccessful team, one with a losing record. Therefore, the system assigns a *weight* to each opponent. This weight is determined in a fair, unbiased, and systematic manner by considering a team's record and the records of its opponents. After the weights are assigned, teams accumulate weighted wins and weighted losses.

Unlike the polls and some of the computers, "Weighted Wins" starts all teams from the same position. Each team begins the season with 0.00 wins and a weight of 1.00. (Since wins in all major sports count 1 win, the weight of 1.00 was chosen for the starting point.) As the season develops, the weight of a team increases or decreases depending on whether the team wins or loses. A weight of 1.20 would indicate a relatively strong team and a weight of .85 would indicate a much weaker team. Weights usually range from a high of approximately 1.45 to a low of .55.

The value of a team's win is determined by its opponent's *weight*. Losses are also weighted and determined in a consistent manner.

During the first sixteen years of the Bowl Championship Series, in eleven of those years, the team with the most "Weighted Wins" actually won the BCS Championship game. In all sixteen years, the BCS Champion came from the top four teams in the Weighted Wins standings. Check out a 16-year summary of Weighted Wins standings.

In fact, when comparing WW with BCS formula components, the WW system does better than all eight of the components at having the national champion rated number one before the title game. It also compares favorably when having both the #1 and #2 teams in the championship game.

You can take a look at how the Weighted Wins standings have compared to the NCAA Selection Committee's picks over the past 7 years.

Note: In 2006, the WW system ranked Florida (12-1) as the #1 team and Ohio State (12-0) as the #2 team. This was the first time that a team with one loss finished with more weighted wins than a no loss team from a BCS conference in over 25 years.

The initial landing page of the Weighted Wins website.

In the figure above, you can see the initial landing page when a user visits the site at http://weightedwins.com. The menu along the left-hand side provides links for the user to learn more about the weighted wins concept and the specific details on how each of the formula components is computed. There are a few resources in the Other Links section that provide comparisons on how weighted wins performs against other existing college football ranking systems. Much of this was discussed in chapter 5.

Results for the year 2015 : 11 games are counted

Click on school name for detailed results

No.	Team	Games	Wins	Losses	IW	FW	WW
1	Clemson	13	13	0	1.120	1.460	11.280
2	Alabama	13	12	1	1.100	1.430	11.210
3	Michigan State	13	12	1	1.110	1.470	10.990
4	Ohio State	12	11	1	1.100	1.220	10.570
5	Oklahoma	12	11	1	1.100	1.330	10.520
6	Iowa	13	12	1	1.100	1.270	10.440
7	Stanford	13	11	2	1.090	1.320	10.100
8	Notre Dame	12	10	2	1.080	1.280	9.810
9	Houston	13	12	1	1.100	1.290	9.730
10	Northwestern	12	10	2	1.070	1.250	9.470
11	Texas Christian	12	10	2	1.070	1.140	8.950
12	North Carolina	13	11	2	1.070	1.100	8.950
13	Florida State	12	10	2	1.070	1.150	8.940
14	Oklahoma State	12	10	2	1.070	1.170	8.890
15	Navy	12	10	2	1.070	1.170	8.850
16	Mississippi	12	9	3	1.050	1.260	8.820
17	Michigan	12	9	3	1.060	1.200	8.740
18	Florida	13	10	3	1.070	1.200	8.700
19	Oregon	12	9	3	1.050	1.180	8.670
20	Louisiana State	11	8	3	1.050	1.270	8.570

The View Standings page of the Weighted Wins website.

The most important link, of course, is the WW Standings, which takes you to a page where you simply choose the year from a drop-down menu and click the View Standings button. This will take you to a page that gives you the full standings for that particular year. If you clicked on 2015, for example, the top of the web page would be like the figure shown above.

As you can from the View Standings page, teams are sorted by default in descending order according to their weighted wins value. If you look at the column headings, each of them is clickable, which allows you to sort the teams by any of seven criteria: (1) team, (2) games, (3) wins, (4) losses, (5) initial weight, (6) final weight, and (7) weighted wins.

Michigan Season Results				
Record: 10-2 Inital Weight: 1.080				
Adjustments to Initial Weight: 0.140 Final Weight: 1.220				
Weighted Wins: 9.750				
Opponent	Result	FW Adj	Opp FW	Value Added
Notre Dame (12-0)	L	0.000	1.310	0.230
Western Michigan (7-5)	W	0.010	1.000	1.000
Southern Methodist (5-7)	W	0.000	0.920	0.920
Nebraska (4-8)	W	0.000	0.950	0.950
Northwestern (8-5)	W	0.030	1.060	1.060
Maryland (5-7)	W	0.000	1.020	1.020
Wisconsin (7-5)	W	0.020	1.040	1.040
Michigan State (7-5)	W	0.020	1.100	1.100
Penn State (9-3)	W	0.060	1.180	1.180
Rutgers (1-11)	W	0.000	0.750	Drop
Indiana (5-7)	W	0.000	1.020	1.020
Ohio State (12-1)	L	0.000	1.310	0.230
	Total:	0.140		9.750
	Close			

The 2018 University of Michigan season schedule with the weighted wins breakdown.

Also note that each school name appears as a button. If you click on that button, you get the full breakdown for that school during that particular season. The preceding web page pops up if you are viewing the 2018 standings and then click on the Michigan button. The website allows you to dig deeper if you are curious about any of the data. For example, Western Michigan had an FW adjustment of 0.01 even though it had a 7–5 record (two more wins than losses). By clicking on the Western Michigan schedule for that season, though, you could see that one of its wins was against a non-Bowl Subdivision team, so Western Michigan only counted six wins with its five losses, producing a 0.01 FW adjustment.

The top of this web page includes five values: (1) the team record, (2) the initial weight, (3) the adjustments to the initial weight, (4) the final weight, and (5) the weighted wins value. The season schedule is included in the order that the teams played. The record of each opponent is given, along with the result of the game, the final weight adjustment, the opponent's final weight, and the contribution that game made to the team's overall weighted wins score.

The Administrative Interface

If you click on the Administration menu link on the Weighted Wins main web page, an authentication screen will pop up. Once the proper credentials are entered, the interface below is displayed:

Administrative Menu

Currently, 11 game(s) are being counted

Update the Number of Games to Count

Upload Yearly Results

View Team Codes

View Conferences

Weighted Wins Home

The Weighted Wins Administrative interface.

The most frequently used tool here is the uploading of yearly results. Game results are stored in a simple text file, one game result per line. Using three-letter codes for each team, a game result is stored as the winning team's code, followed by a space, followed by the losing team's code. Only the winner and loser are stored, as weighted wins does not use the score of the game in its formula. If Central Florida beat Memphis, for example, the game would be stored as thus:

CFL MEM

If Air Force tied Army back in the day, the user would store the game as:

TIE AIR ARM

If the person doing data entry forgets a team code, a link labeled View Team Codes will generate a page like this:

Team Codes and Names

Back to main page

Code	Team
AIR	Air Force
AKR	Akron
AKS	Arkansas State
ALA	Alabama
ARK	Arkansas
ARM	Army
ARZ	Arizona
AST	Appalachian State
AUB	Auburn
AZS	Arizona State
BAL	Ball State
BAY	Baylor
BOI	Boise State

Viewing the team codes.

The user can also access the View Conferences link to see which teams belong to each major conference, although these conference affiliations do not factor in the WW formulas.

What about ties?

There is some cleaning up to do regarding a point we ignored in the earlier chapters. Before 1996, games in college football could end in a tie. We intentionally delayed this talking point earlier since we didn't want to needlessly confuse things. To illustrate how ties are computed using weighted wins, let's take a look at Purdue's 1994 season schedule.

Purdue Season Results				
Record: 4-5-2 Inital Weight: 1.000				
Adjustments to Initial Weight: 0.025 Final Weight: 1.025				
Weighted Wins: 4.532				
Opponent	**Result**	**FW Adj**	**Opp FW**	**Value Added**
Ball State (5-5-1)	W	0.005	1.087	1.087
Illinois (6-5-0)	W	0.010	1.075	1.075
Indiana (6-5-0)	L	0.000	0.975	-0.025
Iowa (5-5-1)	T	0.002	1.075	0.537
Michigan (7-4-0)	L	0.000	1.095	0.095
Michigan State (5-6-0)	L	-0.010	1.030	0.030
Minnesota (3-8-0)	W	0.000	0.930	Drop
Notre Dame (6-4-1)	L	0.000	1.087	0.087
Ohio State (9-3-0)	L	0.000	1.125	0.125
Toledo (6-4-1)	W	0.005	1.017	1.017
Wisconsin (6-4-1)	T	0.012	1.005	0.502
	Total:	0.025		4.532
	Close			

The 1994 Purdue season schedule, used to illustrate ties.

The 1994 Purdue season is interesting since it had two ties. Its final record was 4-5-2. We basically treat a tie like half of a win. Therefore, you could think of Purdue's final record as equivalent to 5-5, since two ties would equal a single win. Therefore, Purdue's final weight is equal to 1.000, the same as a team with a 0.500 record.

As for a tie's contribution to the overall weighted wins value, the team earns one-half of the opponent's final weight. Since Iowa had a final weight of 1.075, Purdue earned half of that, or 0.5375. The tie with Wisconsin contributed 0.5025, or half of Wisconsin's 1.005 final weight.

Number of Games to Count

An important feature of the weighted wins standings has to do with the number of games to count. Since teams do not all play the same number of games, counting each team's top N games evens the playing field. Up until 2001, teams played up to eleven games each, so we counted ten games in the standings. Since then, most teams will play twelve games, so we count eleven in the standings. With conference championship games, many of the top teams will play thirteen games in a year. As noted in earlier chapters, no matter how many games a team plays, all losses are counted in that team's weighted wins score. As a season is in progress, we update weekly the number of games to count for that season using the Administrative menu.

CHAPTER 8

WEIGHTED WINS STANDINGS

1981–2020

The only place success comes before work is in the dictionary.

—Vince Lombardi,
former Green Bay Packers coach

In this chapter, we have provided the top 50 teams in the weighted wins standings over the last forty years. Why fifty teams? Well, that's a nice round number, and it also fits nicely onto one page. Also, with 130 FBS schools, showing the top 50 will basically include the winning teams, or those with a 0.500 record or better.

Why forty years? We decided to go back to 1981 so that readers could see how teams fared in the weighted wins standings throughout the last four decades of college football. In order to do this, we needed to include the weighted wins standings for the final seventeen seasons leading up to the Bowl Championship Series (BCS), beginning in 1998. If you also include the sixteen seasons from the BCS era and the first seven seasons of the College Football Playoff (CFP) era, that gives us a total of forty years.

The Era	The Dates	No. of Seasons
CFP	2014–2020	7 years
BCS	1998–2013	16 years
Pre-BCS	1981–1997	17 years

As you view the yearly standings, notice that we highlighted with the use of italics the eventual national champion for each season.

College Football Playoff Era

2014–2020

Weighted Wins Standings for the Year 2014

No.	Team	G	W	L	IW	FW	WW
1	Florida State	13	13	0	1.120	1.320	11.570
2	Alabama	13	12	1	1.100	1.310	11.120
3	Oregon	13	12	1	1.100	1.360	10.760
4	*Ohio State*	*13*	*12*	*1*	*1.110*	*1.330*	*10.550*
5	Texas Christian	12	11	1	1.090	1.220	9.890
6	Mississippi State	12	10	2	1.070	1.140	9.730
7	Baylor	12	11	1	1.090	1.270	9.590
8	Boise State	13	11	2	1.090	1.280	9.400
9	Mississippi	12	9	3	1.050	1.390	9.180
10	Michigan State	12	10	2	1.070	1.140	9.050
11	UCLA	12	9	3	1.060	1.290	9.010
12	Arizona	13	10	3	1.070	1.280	8.960
13	Georgia Tech	13	10	3	1.060	1.220	8.860
14	Missouri	13	10	3	1.060	1.100	8.610
15	Colorado State	12	10	2	1.070	1.130	8.580
16	Marshall	13	12	1	1.090	1.140	8.480
17	Arizona State	11	8	3	1.050	1.140	8.420
18	Georgia	12	9	3	1.050	1.190	8.340
19	Wisconsin	13	10	3	1.060	1.150	8.320
20	Clemson	13	10	3	1.060	1.120	8.310
21	Kansas State	12	9	3	1.050	1.110	8.280
22	Auburn	12	8	4	1.030	1.190	8.140
23	Louisville	12	9	3	1.050	1.050	7.940
24	Louisiana State	12	8	4	1.030	1.140	7.870
25	Utah	12	8	4	1.030	1.070	7.740
26	Northern Illinois	12	10	2	1.070	1.120	7.670
27	Nebraska	12	9	3	1.050	1.070	7.620
28	Cincinnati	12	9	3	1.060	1.120	7.590
29	Memphis	12	9	3	1.050	1.110	7.550
30	Duke	12	9	3	1.050	1.080	7.530
31	Southern California	12	8	4	1.040	1.140	7.460
32	Air Force	12	9	3	1.050	1.170	7.430
33	Minnesota	12	8	4	1.030	1.080	7.190
34	Oklahoma	12	8	4	1.040	1.070	7.130
35	Georgia Southern	12	9	3	1.050	1.080	7.020
36	Central Florida	12	9	3	1.050	1.030	6.980
37	Texas A&M	12	7	5	1.010	1.060	6.970
38	Utah State	13	9	4	1.040	1.110	6.780
39	Notre Dame	12	7	5	1.020	1.020	6.660
40	West Virginia	12	7	5	1.010	1.110	6.570
41	Arkansas	12	6	6	0.990	1.140	6.560
42	Washington	13	8	5	1.020	1.020	6.540
43	Stanford	12	7	5	1.010	1.090	6.540
44	Louisiana-Lafayette	12	8	4	1.030	1.060	6.510
45	Rutgers	12	7	5	1.010	1.020	6.490
46	Maryland	12	7	5	1.010	1.020	6.490
47	Brigham Young	12	8	4	1.030	1.040	6.440
48	East Carolina	12	8	4	1.030	1.010	6.280
49	Boston College	12	7	5	1.010	1.040	6.170
50	Tennessee	12	6	6	0.990	1.040	6.150

Weighted Wins Standings for the Year 2015

No.	Team	G	W	L	IW	FW	WW
1	Clemson	13	13	0	1.120	1.460	11.280
2	*Alabama*	13	12	1	1.100	1.430	11.210
3	Michigan State	13	12	1	1.110	1.470	10.990
4	Ohio State	12	11	1	1.100	1.220	10.570
5	Oklahoma	12	11	1	1.100	1.330	10.520
6	Iowa	13	12	1	1.100	1.270	10.440
7	Stanford	13	11	2	1.090	1.320	10.100
8	Notre Dame	12	10	2	1.080	1.280	9.810
9	Houston	13	12	1	1.100	1.290	9.730
10	Northwestern	12	10	2	1.070	1.250	9.470
11	Texas Christian	12	10	2	1.070	1.140	8.950
12	North Carolina	13	11	2	1.070	1.100	8.950
13	Florida State	12	10	2	1.070	1.150	8.940
14	Oklahoma State	12	10	2	1.070	1.170	8.890
15	Navy	12	10	2	1.070	1.170	8.850
16	Mississippi	12	9	3	1.050	1.260	8.820
17	Michigan	12	9	3	1.060	1.200	8.740
18	Florida	13	10	3	1.070	1.200	8.700
19	Oregon	12	9	3	1.050	1.180	8.670
20	Louisiana State	11	8	3	1.050	1.270	8.570
21	Utah	12	9	3	1.060	1.170	8.510
22	Western Kentucky	13	11	2	1.090	1.180	8.450
23	Toledo	11	9	2	1.070	1.210	8.330
24	Bowling Green	13	10	3	1.070	1.150	8.240
25	Memphis	12	9	3	1.050	1.210	8.100
26	Wisconsin	12	9	3	1.060	1.060	8.070
27	Brigham Young	12	9	3	1.050	1.060	8.040
28	Temple	13	10	3	1.060	1.140	8.000
29	Mississippi State	12	8	4	1.030	1.100	7.880
30	Georgia	12	9	3	1.050	1.080	7.860
31	Appalachian State	12	10	2	1.070	1.100	7.830
32	Baylor	12	9	3	1.050	1.120	7.800
33	Texas A&M	12	8	4	1.030	1.060	7.640
34	Southern California	13	8	5	1.030	1.180	7.590
35	Tennessee	12	8	4	1.030	1.150	7.470
36	UCLA	12	8	4	1.040	1.150	7.400
37	Miami-Florida	12	8	4	1.030	1.080	7.350
38	Pittsburgh	13	9	4	1.040	1.070	7.320
39	Arkansas	12	7	5	1.010	1.140	7.280
40	San Diego State	13	10	3	1.060	1.060	7.040
41	California	12	7	5	1.010	1.110	7.010
42	Penn State	12	7	5	1.020	1.080	6.960
43	South Florida Univ	12	8	4	1.030	1.030	6.830
44	Arkansas State	12	9	3	1.050	1.090	6.790
45	Ohio University	12	8	4	1.030	1.050	6.660
46	Western Michigan	13	8	5	1.020	1.130	6.400
47	Louisville	12	7	5	1.010	1.010	6.390
48	West Virginia	12	7	5	1.010	1.040	6.350
49	Washington State	12	8	4	1.040	1.020	6.350
50	Texas Tech	12	7	5	1.010	1.020	6.330

Weighted Wins Standings for the Year 2016

No.	Team	G	W	L	IW	FW	WW
1	Alabama	13	13	0	1.120	1.410	11.900
2	Ohio State	12	11	1	1.100	1.440	10.940
3	*Clemson*	*13*	*12*	*1*	*1.100*	*1.340*	*10.570*
4	Western Michigan	13	13	0	1.120	1.210	10.210
5	Penn State	13	11	2	1.090	1.390	10.050
6	Washington	13	12	1	1.100	1.310	10.020
7	Michigan	12	10	2	1.080	1.300	9.770
8	Oklahoma	12	10	2	1.080	1.230	9.200
9	South Florida Univ	12	10	2	1.070	1.150	8.790
10	Boise State	12	10	2	1.080	1.190	8.780
11	Wisconsin	13	10	3	1.070	1.220	8.770
12	West Virginia	12	10	2	1.070	1.130	8.550
13	Colorado	13	10	3	1.060	1.200	8.500
14	Nebraska	12	9	3	1.060	1.110	8.370
15	Southern California	12	9	3	1.060	1.220	8.360
16	Navy	12	9	3	1.050	1.180	8.070
17	Louisville	12	9	3	1.060	1.110	8.010
18	Stanford	12	9	3	1.060	1.150	7.990
19	Tulsa	12	9	3	1.050	1.080	7.940
20	Temple	13	10	3	1.060	1.170	7.940
21	Houston	12	9	3	1.050	1.210	7.830
22	Oklahoma State	12	9	3	1.050	1.160	7.670
23	Tennessee	12	8	4	1.030	1.190	7.670
24	Florida	12	8	4	1.040	1.080	7.650
25	Western Kentucky	13	10	3	1.060	1.160	7.630
26	Florida State	11	8	3	1.040	1.180	7.610
27	Auburn	12	8	4	1.030	1.070	7.580
28	Appalachian State	12	9	3	1.060	1.130	7.420
29	Texas A&M	12	8	4	1.030	1.050	7.370
30	San Diego State	13	10	3	1.060	1.060	7.320
31	Pittsburgh	12	8	4	1.030	1.230	7.300
32	Memphis	12	8	4	1.030	1.120	7.210
33	Minnesota	12	8	4	1.030	1.040	7.190
34	Toledo	11	8	3	1.050	1.080	7.110
35	Virginia Tech	11	8	3	1.040	1.060	6.970
36	Utah	12	8	4	1.030	1.050	6.940
37	Old Dominion	12	9	3	1.050	1.040	6.730
38	Air Force	12	9	3	1.050	1.170	6.630
39	Louisiana State	11	7	4	1.020	1.060	6.630
40	Brigham Young	12	8	4	1.030	1.050	6.570
41	Kansas State	12	8	4	1.030	1.030	6.550
42	Kentucky	12	7	5	1.010	1.060	6.540
43	New Mexico	12	8	4	1.030	0.950	6.540
44	Iowa	12	8	4	1.040	1.120	6.410
45	Troy State	12	9	3	1.050	1.100	6.380
46	Washington State	12	8	4	1.040	1.020	6.360
47	Georgia	12	7	5	1.010	1.040	6.300
48	Arkansas	12	7	5	1.010	1.010	6.300
49	Wyoming	13	8	5	1.020	1.160	6.240
50	Colorado State	12	7	5	1.010	1.100	6.100

Weighted Wins Standings for the Year 2017

No.	Team	G	W	L	IW	FW	WW
1	Clemson	13	12	1	1.100	1.350	10.930
2	Central Florida	12	12	0	1.110	1.360	10.880
3	Georgia	13	12	1	1.100	1.330	10.840
4	Oklahoma	13	12	1	1.110	1.400	10.720
5	Wisconsin	13	12	1	1.110	1.290	10.480
6	*Alabama*	12	11	1	1.090	1.230	10.340
7	Southern California	13	11	2	1.090	1.220	9.870
8	Ohio State	13	11	2	1.090	1.430	9.790
9	Miami-Florida	12	10	2	1.070	1.230	9.490
10	Penn State	12	10	2	1.080	1.210	9.350
11	Washington	12	10	2	1.070	1.170	9.260
12	Notre Dame	12	9	3	1.060	1.270	9.140
13	Memphis	12	10	2	1.070	1.110	9.110
14	Auburn	13	10	3	1.060	1.300	9.100
15	Texas Christian	13	10	3	1.060	1.150	8.740
16	Michigan State	12	9	3	1.060	1.200	8.670
17	Toledo	13	11	2	1.080	1.140	8.550
18	San Diego State	12	10	2	1.070	1.170	8.460
19	Washington State	12	9	3	1.050	1.240	8.370
20	Louisiana State	12	9	3	1.050	1.120	8.320
21	Florida Atlantic	13	10	3	1.060	1.180	8.280
22	Boise State	13	10	3	1.070	1.260	8.280
23	Stanford	13	9	4	1.050	1.210	8.230
24	Virginia Tech	12	9	3	1.050	1.060	8.140
25	Northwestern	12	9	3	1.060	1.130	8.060
26	South Florida Univ	12	10	2	1.070	1.070	8.010
27	Oklahoma State	12	9	3	1.060	1.080	7.920
28	Army	12	9	3	1.050	1.020	7.910
29	Troy State	12	10	2	1.070	1.100	7.800
30	North Carolina State	12	8	4	1.030	1.100	7.650
31	South Carolina	12	8	4	1.030	1.070	7.550
32	Michigan	12	8	4	1.040	1.040	7.490
33	Mississippi State	12	8	4	1.030	1.090	7.410
34	Iowa	12	7	5	1.020	1.170	7.270
35	Louisville	12	8	4	1.030	1.040	7.270
36	North Texas	13	9	4	1.040	1.150	7.050
37	Fresno State	13	9	4	1.040	1.170	6.920
38	Boston College	12	7	5	1.020	1.110	6.910
39	Wake Forest	12	7	5	1.010	1.080	6.780
40	Arizona State	12	7	5	1.020	1.090	6.700
41	Houston	11	7	4	1.030	0.990	6.700
42	Northern Illinois	12	8	4	1.030	1.030	6.630
43	Florida International	12	8	4	1.030	1.020	6.570
44	Oregon	12	7	5	1.010	1.030	6.420
45	Central Michigan	12	8	4	1.030	1.010	6.410
46	Iowa State	12	7	5	1.010	1.180	6.360
47	Texas A&M	12	7	5	1.010	1.040	6.350
48	West Virginia	12	7	5	1.010	1.030	6.310
49	Kentucky	12	7	5	1.010	1.040	6.270
50	Southern Methodist	12	7	5	1.010	1.070	6.180

Weighted Wins Standings for the Year 2018

No.	Team	G	W	L	IW	FW	WW
1	Alabama	13	13	0	1.120	1.380	11.770
2	*Clemson*	*13*	*13*	*0*	*1.120*	*1.340*	*11.750*
3	Notre Dame	12	12	0	1.120	1.310	11.370
4	Central Florida	12	12	0	1.110	1.270	10.510
5	Ohio State	13	12	1	1.110	1.310	10.500
6	Oklahoma	13	12	1	1.110	1.280	10.330
7	Georgia	13	11	2	1.080	1.250	10.060
8	Michigan	12	10	2	1.080	1.220	9.750
9	Fresno State	13	11	2	1.090	1.200	9.160
10	Washington State	12	10	2	1.070	1.160	8.740
11	Cincinnati	12	10	2	1.070	1.110	8.670
12	Appalachian State	12	10	2	1.070	1.150	8.540
13	Louisiana State	12	9	3	1.050	1.190	8.520
14	Florida	12	9	3	1.050	1.140	8.430
15	Penn State	12	9	3	1.060	1.180	8.410
16	Kentucky	12	9	3	1.050	1.150	8.310
17	Washington	13	10	3	1.060	1.260	8.310
18	Boise State	13	10	3	1.070	1.280	8.230
19	Syracuse	12	9	3	1.050	1.120	8.050
20	Utah State	12	10	2	1.070	1.090	8.030
21	Texas A&M	12	8	4	1.030	1.200	7.920
22	North Carolina State	12	9	3	1.050	1.090	7.910
23	Missouri	12	8	4	1.030	1.100	7.790
24	Mississippi State	12	8	4	1.030	1.080	7.730
25	Utah	13	9	4	1.040	1.120	7.700
26	Stanford	12	8	4	1.030	1.090	7.680
27	Univ Alabama-Birmingham	13	10	3	1.060	1.100	7.650
28	Troy State	12	9	3	1.050	1.080	7.560
29	Buffalo	13	10	3	1.060	1.130	7.530
30	Georgia Southern	12	9	3	1.050	1.140	7.400
31	Texas	13	9	4	1.050	1.160	7.370
32	Iowa	12	8	4	1.030	1.090	7.340
33	Army	11	9	2	1.050	1.150	7.060
34	West Virginia	11	8	3	1.040	1.080	7.020
35	Northwestern	13	8	5	1.030	1.060	7.020
36	Iowa State	12	8	4	1.030	1.060	7.020
37	Auburn	12	7	5	1.010	1.070	7.010
38	South Carolina	12	7	5	1.010	1.040	6.980
39	Oregon	12	8	4	1.030	1.090	6.790
40	Michigan State	12	7	5	1.020	1.100	6.700
41	Ohio University	12	8	4	1.030	1.100	6.540
42	Boston College	12	7	5	1.010	1.030	6.530
43	North Texas	12	9	3	1.050	1.000	6.490
44	Duke	12	7	5	1.010	1.090	6.460
45	Arkansas State	12	8	4	1.030	1.030	6.340
46	Pittsburgh	13	7	6	1.000	1.000	6.300
47	Marshall	12	8	4	1.030	1.050	6.270
48	Georgia Tech	12	7	5	1.010	1.030	6.260
49	Northern Illinois	13	8	5	1.020	1.090	6.230
50	Arizona State	12	7	5	1.020	1.050	6.200

Weighted Wins Standings for the Year 2019

No.	Team	G	W	L	IW	FW	WW
1	Ohio State	13	13	0	1.130	1.580	12.300
2	*Louisiana State*	*13*	*13*	*0*	*1.120*	*1.430*	*11.780*
3	Clemson	13	13	0	1.120	1.220	10.850
4	Memphis	13	12	1	1.100	1.390	10.450
5	Oklahoma	13	12	1	1.100	1.320	10.060
6	Boise State	13	12	1	1.100	1.280	9.890
7	Appalachian State	13	12	1	1.100	1.240	9.790
8	Penn State	12	10	2	1.070	1.240	9.750
9	Georgia	13	11	2	1.080	1.260	9.570
10	Notre Dame	12	10	2	1.080	1.260	9.570
11	Wisconsin	13	10	3	1.070	1.290	9.360
12	Cincinnati	13	10	3	1.070	1.200	9.220
13	Baylor	13	11	2	1.080	1.170	9.170
14	Alabama	12	10	2	1.070	1.100	9.100
15	Oregon	13	11	2	1.080	1.220	9.030
16	Michigan	12	9	3	1.060	1.230	9.020
17	Navy	12	10	2	1.070	1.220	8.980
18	Southern Methodist	12	10	2	1.080	1.120	8.940
19	Minnesota	12	10	2	1.070	1.150	8.920
20	Utah	13	11	2	1.080	1.120	8.900
21	Auburn	12	9	3	1.050	1.210	8.780
22	Air Force	12	10	2	1.070	1.120	8.680
23	Florida	12	10	2	1.060	1.130	8.440
24	Florida Atlantic	13	10	3	1.060	1.160	8.340
25	Iowa	12	9	3	1.060	1.160	8.300
26	Louisiana-Lafayette	13	10	3	1.060	1.070	7.950
27	Central Florida	12	9	3	1.050	1.100	7.600
28	Southern California	12	8	4	1.040	1.140	7.170
29	Virginia	13	9	4	1.040	1.060	7.080
30	Oklahoma State	12	8	4	1.030	1.020	7.080
31	Kansas State	12	8	4	1.030	1.110	7.070
32	San Diego State	12	9	3	1.050	1.070	7.030
33	Indiana	12	8	4	1.030	1.030	7.030
34	Marshall	12	8	4	1.030	1.130	6.920
35	Temple	12	8	4	1.030	1.130	6.810
36	Wake Forest	12	8	4	1.030	1.010	6.700
37	Texas A&M	12	7	5	1.010	1.010	6.700
38	Louisiana Tech	12	9	3	1.050	1.060	6.650
39	Texas	12	7	5	1.020	1.100	6.620
40	Utah State	12	7	5	1.010	1.070	6.500
41	Miami-Ohio	13	8	5	1.020	1.030	6.500
42	Iowa State	12	7	5	1.010	1.030	6.370
43	Tennessee	12	7	5	1.010	1.060	6.280
44	Hawaii	14	9	5	1.030	1.030	6.140
45	Washington	12	7	5	1.010	1.030	6.130
46	Louisville	12	7	5	1.010	1.100	6.060
47	Georgia Southern	12	7	5	1.010	1.090	6.020
48	Michigan State	12	6	6	1.000	1.040	6.020
49	Central Michigan	12	8	4	1.030	1.020	6.000
50	Arizona State	12	7	5	1.010	1.010	6.000

Weighted Wins Standings for the Year 2020

No.	Team	G	W	L	IW	FW	WW
1	*Alabama*	11	11	0	1.110	1.290	10.910
2	Coastal Carolina	11	11	0	1.100	1.320	9.830
3	Notre Dame	11	10	1	1.090	1.220	9.720
4	Clemson	11	10	1	1.080	1.240	9.170
5	Brigham Young	11	10	1	1.080	1.120	9.080
6	Louisiana-Lafayette	10	9	1	1.080	1.210	8.910
7	Iowa State	11	8	3	1.050	1.150	8.300
8	Miami-Florida	10	8	2	1.060	1.130	8.130
9	Cincinnati	9	9	0	1.080	1.230	8.120
10	Texas A&M	9	8	1	1.070	1.140	7.770
11	Florida	11	8	3	1.050	1.090	7.740
12	North Carolina State	11	8	3	1.050	1.100	7.600
13	Oklahoma	10	8	2	1.050	1.170	7.110
14	Oklahoma State	10	7	3	1.040	1.130	7.070
15	San Jose State	7	7	0	1.070	1.140	6.940
16	North Carolina	11	8	3	1.040	1.110	6.900
17	Appalachian State	11	8	3	1.040	1.060	6.810
18	Liberty	10	9	1	1.060	1.060	6.300
19	Texas	9	6	3	1.030	1.070	6.170
20	Tulsa	8	6	2	1.040	1.100	6.170
21	Texas Christian	10	6	4	1.020	1.070	6.090
22	Ball State	7	6	1	1.050	1.120	6.040
23	Georgia Southern	12	7	5	1.010	1.020	6.020
24	Central Florida	9	6	3	1.030	1.040	5.900
25	Marshall	9	7	2	1.040	1.080	5.900
26	Tulane	11	6	5	1.010	1.020	5.890
27	Boston College	11	6	5	1.010	0.990	5.890
28	Georgia	8	6	2	1.040	1.050	5.890
29	Ohio State	6	6	0	1.060	1.150	5.840
30	Northwestern	8	6	2	1.040	1.050	5.830
31	Indiana	7	6	1	1.050	1.050	5.810
32	Memphis	10	7	3	1.030	1.060	5.790
33	Nevada	8	6	2	1.040	1.040	5.790
34	Iowa	8	6	2	1.040	1.020	5.670
35	Virginia Tech	11	5	6	0.990	1.040	5.410
36	Univ Alabama-Birmingham	8	5	3	1.020	1.070	5.280
37	Pittsburgh	11	6	5	1.000	1.000	5.230
38	Boise State	7	5	2	1.030	1.030	5.090
39	Auburn	9	5	4	1.010	0.950	5.090
40	Southern Methodist	9	6	3	1.020	1.030	5.050
41	Georgia State	9	5	4	1.010	0.980	4.970
42	Louisiana State	9	5	4	1.010	1.030	4.960
43	Southern California	6	5	1	1.040	1.050	4.920
44	Army	9	7	2	1.030	1.050	4.900
45	Univ of Texas at San Ant	10	6	4	1.010	1.010	4.890
46	Virginia	10	5	5	0.990	1.020	4.360
47	San Diego State	8	4	4	1.000	1.000	4.230
48	Kansas State	10	4	6	0.980	0.960	4.220
49	Louisiana Tech	8	4	4	1.000	1.020	4.140
50	Louisville	11	4	7	0.970	0.910	4.130

Bowl Championship
Series (BCS) Era
1998–2013

Weighted Wins Standings for the Year 1998

No.	Team	G	W	L	IW	FW	WW
1	*Tennessee*	*12*	*12*	*0*	*1.120*	*1.430*	*10.620*
2	Florida State	12	11	1	1.100	1.480	9.860
3	UCLA	11	10	1	1.090	1.340	9.600
4	Kansas State	12	11	1	1.090	1.250	9.310
5	Ohio State	11	10	1	1.090	1.280	9.170
6	Tulane	11	11	0	1.110	1.160	9.130
7	Arizona	12	11	1	1.100	1.190	9.120
8	Texas A&M	13	11	2	1.090	1.320	9.020
9	Wisconsin	11	10	1	1.090	1.210	8.810
10	Florida	11	9	2	1.060	1.140	8.650
11	Air Force	12	11	1	1.100	1.220	8.610
12	Notre Dame	11	9	2	1.070	1.170	8.260
13	Arkansas	11	9	2	1.070	1.110	8.160
14	Miami-Ohio	11	10	1	1.090	1.110	8.140
15	Virginia	11	9	2	1.070	1.160	8.100
16	Georgia Tech	11	9	2	1.070	1.200	8.000
17	Texas	11	8	3	1.050	1.200	7.770
18	Marshall	12	11	1	1.080	1.170	7.750
19	Nebraska	12	9	3	1.060	1.120	7.630
20	Michigan	12	9	3	1.060	1.200	7.520
21	Penn State	11	8	3	1.050	1.120	7.510
22	Oregon	11	8	3	1.050	1.090	7.480
23	Syracuse	11	8	3	1.050	1.200	7.450
24	Georgia	11	8	3	1.050	1.100	7.420
25	Miami-Florida	11	8	3	1.040	1.180	7.320
26	Mississippi State	12	9	3	1.050	1.120	7.310
27	Southern California	12	8	4	1.040	1.180	7.100
28	Wyoming	11	8	3	1.040	1.080	6.930
29	West Virginia	11	8	3	1.050	1.100	6.910
30	Missouri	11	7	4	1.020	1.080	6.900
31	Virginia Tech	11	8	3	1.050	1.070	6.870
32	Alabama	11	7	4	1.030	1.110	6.760
33	Purdue	12	8	4	1.040	1.090	6.390
34	North Carolina State	11	7	4	1.030	1.110	6.360
35	Texas Tech	11	7	4	1.030	1.070	6.340
36	Colorado	11	7	4	1.030	1.060	6.210
37	San Diego State	11	7	4	1.030	1.060	6.150
38	Colorado State	12	8	4	1.040	1.040	6.120
39	Southern Mississippi	11	7	4	1.030	1.050	6.090
40	Brigham Young	13	9	4	1.040	1.090	5.900
41	Central Florida	11	9	2	1.050	1.010	5.880
42	Washington	11	6	5	1.010	1.050	5.850
43	Kentucky	11	6	5	1.000	1.020	5.630
44	Louisville	11	7	4	1.020	1.020	5.540
45	Utah	11	7	4	1.030	1.030	5.470
46	North Carolina	11	6	5	1.010	0.990	5.230
47	Texas Christian	11	6	5	1.010	1.070	5.090
48	Mississippi	11	6	5	1.010	0.960	4.980
49	Oklahoma State	11	5	6	0.990	1.000	4.910
50	Toledo	11	6	5	1.010	0.990	4.870

Weighted Wins Standings for the Year 1999

No.	Team	G	W	L	IW	FW	WW
1	*Florida State*	11	11	0	1.110	1.340	10.380
2	Virginia Tech	11	11	0	1.100	1.220	9.760
3	Nebraska	12	11	1	1.100	1.340	9.600
4	Marshall	12	12	0	1.110	1.170	9.250
5	Kansas State	11	10	1	1.090	1.150	8.990
6	Alabama	12	10	2	1.080	1.410	8.970
7	Tennessee	11	9	2	1.070	1.210	8.750
8	Michigan	11	9	2	1.070	1.230	8.660
9	Michigan State	11	9	2	1.070	1.280	8.610
10	Mississippi State	11	9	2	1.070	1.110	8.340
11	Florida	12	9	3	1.060	1.170	8.240
12	Wisconsin	11	9	2	1.060	1.150	8.050
13	Penn State	12	9	3	1.060	1.180	7.820
14	East Carolina	11	9	2	1.070	1.130	7.720
15	Southern Mississippi	11	8	3	1.040	1.130	7.450
16	Texas A&M	11	8	3	1.050	1.180	7.320
17	Stanford	11	8	3	1.050	1.030	7.270
18	Oregon	11	8	3	1.050	1.050	7.220
19	Brigham Young	12	9	3	1.060	1.140	7.170
20	Louisiana Tech	11	8	3	1.040	1.120	7.110
21	Minnesota	11	8	3	1.040	1.130	7.040
22	Georgia Tech	11	8	3	1.050	1.090	7.000
23	Utah	11	8	3	1.050	1.110	6.960
24	Colorado State	11	8	3	1.050	1.110	6.920
25	Texas	13	9	4	1.050	1.220	6.860
26	Purdue	11	7	4	1.030	1.140	6.750
27	Houston	12	8	4	1.040	1.030	6.710
28	Illinois	11	7	4	1.030	1.080	6.600
29	Miami-Florida	12	8	4	1.030	1.080	6.550
30	Boston College	11	8	3	1.040	0.980	6.450
31	Arkansas	11	7	4	1.030	1.120	6.440
32	Mississippi	11	7	4	1.030	1.050	6.420
33	Virginia	11	7	4	1.030	1.100	6.320
34	Boise State	12	9	3	1.040	1.000	6.310
35	Georgia	11	7	4	1.030	1.040	6.290
36	Washington	11	7	4	1.030	1.120	6.250
37	Wyoming	11	7	4	1.020	1.070	6.150
38	Oregon State	11	7	4	1.020	1.050	6.110
39	Oklahoma	11	7	4	1.020	1.060	5.970
40	Fresno State	12	8	4	1.030	1.070	5.750
41	Hawaii	12	8	4	1.030	1.030	5.620
42	Clemson	11	6	5	1.010	1.040	5.510
43	Kentucky	11	6	5	1.000	1.030	5.440
44	Texas Christian	11	7	4	1.030	1.000	5.410
45	Colorado	11	6	5	1.010	1.030	5.340
46	Miami-Ohio	11	7	4	1.030	0.970	5.330
47	Ohio State	12	6	6	1.000	1.070	5.290
48	Memphis	11	6	5	1.010	1.020	5.270
49	Louisville	12	7	5	1.010	1.010	5.190
50	Auburn	11	5	6	0.980	1.020	5.090

Weighted Wins Standings for the Year 2000

No.	Team	G	W	L	IW	FW	WW
1	*Oklahoma*	*12*	*12*	*0*	*1.120*	*1.500*	*10.630*
2	Florida State	12	11	1	1.100	1.400	10.130
3	Washington	11	10	1	1.090	1.270	9.500
4	Miami-Florida	11	10	1	1.080	1.320	9.380
5	Virginia Tech	11	10	1	1.090	1.180	9.370
6	Oregon State	11	10	1	1.080	1.160	9.110
7	Florida	12	10	2	1.080	1.320	8.890
8	Nebraska	11	9	2	1.070	1.220	8.540
9	Notre Dame	11	9	2	1.070	1.190	8.500
10	Oregon	11	9	2	1.070	1.180	8.220
11	Georgia Tech	11	9	2	1.070	1.160	8.220
12	Clemson	11	9	2	1.060	1.130	8.040
13	Kansas State	13	10	3	1.070	1.210	7.950
14	Texas Christian	11	10	1	1.090	1.220	7.940
15	Auburn	12	9	3	1.060	1.130	7.860
16	Texas	11	9	2	1.070	1.110	7.820
17	Ohio State	11	8	3	1.050	1.130	7.410
18	Northwestern	11	8	3	1.050	1.090	7.400
19	Tennessee	11	8	3	1.050	1.100	7.310
20	Purdue	11	8	3	1.050	1.220	7.220
21	Michigan	11	8	3	1.050	1.140	7.200
22	Western Michigan	11	9	2	1.060	1.080	7.200
23	Colorado State	11	9	2	1.060	1.080	7.140
24	Iowa State	11	8	3	1.050	1.090	6.950
25	Toledo	11	10	1	1.070	1.070	6.950
26	Louisville	11	9	2	1.050	1.130	6.930
27	Texas El-Paso	11	8	3	1.050	1.090	6.890
28	Wisconsin	12	8	4	1.040	1.210	6.690
29	Texas A&M	11	7	4	1.030	1.170	6.640
30	Louisiana State	11	7	4	1.020	1.130	6.590
31	Mississippi State	11	7	4	1.030	1.170	6.520
32	South Carolina	11	7	4	1.030	1.030	6.400
33	Georgia	11	7	4	1.020	1.100	6.390
34	Mississippi	11	7	4	1.030	1.040	6.270
35	Pittsburgh	11	7	4	1.030	1.040	6.170
36	Air Force	11	8	3	1.040	1.070	6.050
37	Cincinnati	11	7	4	1.030	1.040	6.040
38	Southern Mississippi	11	7	4	1.020	1.050	5.950
39	East Carolina	11	7	4	1.030	1.090	5.920
40	North Carolina State	11	7	4	1.030	1.100	5.860
41	West Virginia	11	6	5	1.010	1.040	5.720
42	UCLA	11	6	5	1.010	1.030	5.670
43	Boise State	11	9	2	1.050	1.020	5.630
44	Fresno State	11	7	4	1.030	1.040	5.550
45	Virginia	11	6	5	1.000	1.040	5.530
46	Syracuse	11	6	5	1.010	1.050	5.510
47	Texas Tech	12	7	5	1.020	1.020	5.470
48	North Carolina	11	6	5	1.010	1.040	5.440
49	Univ Alabama-Birmingham	11	7	4	1.020	1.030	5.340
50	Arizona State	11	6	5	1.010	1.040	5.260

Weighted Wins Standings for the Year 2001

No.	Team	G	W	L	IW	FW	WW
1	*Miami-Florida*	*11*	*11*	*0*	*1.110*	*1.320*	*10.480*
2	Nebraska	12	11	1	1.100	1.280	9.480
3	Oregon	11	10	1	1.090	1.220	9.300
4	Tennessee	12	10	2	1.080	1.340	9.250
5	Illinois	11	10	1	1.090	1.200	9.140
6	Colorado	12	10	2	1.080	1.320	8.920
7	Florida	11	9	2	1.070	1.310	8.900
8	Maryland	11	10	1	1.090	1.140	8.900
9	Brigham Young	13	12	1	1.110	1.160	8.650
10	Texas	12	10	2	1.080	1.210	8.640
11	Fresno State	13	11	2	1.090	1.250	8.530
12	Stanford	11	9	2	1.070	1.230	8.500
13	Washington State	11	9	2	1.060	1.200	8.420
14	Oklahoma	12	10	2	1.080	1.180	8.410
15	Louisiana State	12	9	3	1.060	1.240	8.150
16	Syracuse	12	9	3	1.060	1.160	7.830
17	South Carolina	11	8	3	1.040	1.140	7.770
18	Washington	11	8	3	1.050	1.220	7.740
19	Marshall	12	10	2	1.060	1.130	7.710
20	Georgia	11	8	3	1.050	1.180	7.660
21	Louisville	12	10	2	1.070	1.110	7.660
22	Michigan	11	8	3	1.050	1.180	7.380
23	Hawaii	12	9	3	1.050	1.220	7.150
24	Toledo	11	9	2	1.070	1.110	7.080
25	Arkansas	11	7	4	1.020	1.110	7.000
26	Auburn	11	7	4	1.030	1.200	6.940
27	Florida State	11	7	4	1.030	1.130	6.870
28	Virginia Tech	11	8	3	1.040	1.070	6.840
29	UCLA	11	7	4	1.030	1.120	6.780
30	Bowling Green	11	8	3	1.050	1.100	6.750
31	Texas Tech	11	7	4	1.020	1.000	6.430
32	Texas A&M	11	7	4	1.020	1.050	6.400
33	Louisiana Tech	11	7	4	1.030	1.070	6.240
34	Iowa State	11	7	4	1.020	1.030	6.210
35	Ohio State	11	7	4	1.030	1.050	6.210
36	Boise State	12	8	4	1.040	1.180	6.150
37	Mississippi	11	7	4	1.020	1.080	6.110
38	Boston College	11	7	4	1.030	1.030	6.090
39	Rice	12	8	4	1.040	1.100	6.070
40	North Carolina State	11	7	4	1.030	1.060	6.050
41	Alabama	11	6	5	1.010	1.070	5.970
42	Utah	11	7	4	1.030	1.040	5.840
43	Kansas State	11	6	5	1.010	1.070	5.820
44	Middle Tennessee	11	8	3	1.040	1.030	5.820
45	North Carolina	11	6	5	1.010	1.070	5.780
46	Southern California	11	6	5	1.010	1.030	5.630
47	Colorado State	11	6	5	1.010	0.990	5.480
48	Georgia Tech	12	7	5	1.010	1.090	5.440
49	Cincinnati	11	7	4	1.020	1.020	5.390
50	Miami-Ohio	12	7	5	1.020	1.090	5.330

Weighted Wins Standings for the Year 2002

No.	Team	G	W	L	IW	FW	WW
1	*Ohio State*	13	13	0	1.130	1.380	11.510
2	Miami-Florida	12	12	0	1.110	1.420	11.460
3	Georgia	13	12	1	1.100	1.370	11.130
4	Southern California	12	10	2	1.080	1.360	10.340
5	Oklahoma	13	11	2	1.090	1.420	10.060
6	Iowa	12	11	1	1.100	1.260	9.950
7	Texas	12	10	2	1.080	1.170	9.650
8	Notre Dame	12	10	2	1.080	1.330	9.590
9	Washington State	12	10	2	1.070	1.220	9.450
10	Alabama	13	10	3	1.070	1.270	9.220
11	Michigan	12	9	3	1.060	1.160	8.940
12	Boise State	12	11	1	1.100	1.190	8.830
13	Colorado	13	9	4	1.050	1.160	8.660
14	Maryland	13	10	3	1.060	1.200	8.640
15	Florida State	13	9	4	1.050	1.220	8.630
16	Penn State	12	9	3	1.060	1.110	8.480
17	West Virginia	12	9	3	1.050	1.190	8.430
18	Kansas State	12	10	2	1.060	1.150	8.250
19	Arkansas	13	9	4	1.050	1.260	8.180
20	North Carolina State	13	10	3	1.050	1.150	8.170
21	Florida	12	8	4	1.040	1.230	8.100
22	Colorado State	13	10	3	1.070	1.190	8.090
23	Auburn	12	8	4	1.030	1.130	7.930
24	Virginia Tech	13	9	4	1.050	1.170	7.910
25	Pittsburgh	12	8	4	1.040	1.170	7.900
26	Louisiana State	12	8	4	1.030	1.110	7.870
27	Marshall	12	10	2	1.070	1.090	7.860
28	Tennessee	12	8	4	1.040	1.110	7.790
29	Texas Christian	11	9	2	1.070	1.080	7.700
30	Oregon State	12	8	4	1.030	1.090	7.520
31	Hawaii	13	10	3	1.060	1.080	7.460
32	Texas Tech	13	8	5	1.030	1.120	7.400
33	South Florida Univ	11	9	2	1.050	1.160	7.350
34	Boston College	12	8	4	1.040	1.120	7.260
35	UCLA	12	7	5	1.020	1.150	7.060
36	Bowling Green	12	9	3	1.050	1.050	7.060
37	Virginia	13	8	5	1.030	1.160	7.030
38	Toledo	13	9	4	1.040	1.140	6.960
39	Clemson	12	7	5	1.020	1.040	6.940
40	Georgia Tech	12	7	5	1.020	1.100	6.700
41	Washington	12	7	5	1.020	1.130	6.630
42	Arizona State	13	8	5	1.020	1.030	6.610
43	California	12	7	5	1.020	1.050	6.550
44	Air Force	12	8	4	1.040	0.920	6.540
45	Oklahoma State	12	7	5	1.010	1.060	6.490
46	Oregon	12	7	5	1.010	1.060	6.450
47	Kentucky	12	7	5	1.020	1.070	6.370
48	Iowa State	13	7	6	1.000	1.120	6.140
49	Minnesota	12	7	5	1.010	1.040	6.080
50	Miami-Ohio	12	7	5	1.020	1.070	6.070

Weighted Wins Standings for the Year 2003

No.	Team	G	W	L	IW	FW	WW
1	Oklahoma	13	12	1	1.110	1.370	10.800
2	*Louisiana State*	*13*	*12*	*1*	*1.100*	*1.350*	*10.730*
3	*Southern California*	*12*	*11*	*1*	*1.100*	*1.200*	*10.380*
4	Ohio State	12	10	2	1.080	1.300	10.220
5	Miami-Ohio	13	12	1	1.110	1.250	10.150
6	Texas	12	10	2	1.080	1.270	9.770
7	Michigan	12	10	2	1.080	1.340	9.720
8	Florida State	12	10	2	1.080	1.190	9.700
9	Miami-Florida	12	10	2	1.080	1.290	9.700
10	Texas Christian	12	11	1	1.100	1.220	9.380
11	Tennessee	12	10	2	1.080	1.240	9.370
12	Boise State	13	12	1	1.100	1.170	9.030
13	Georgia	13	10	3	1.070	1.190	8.970
14	Purdue	12	9	3	1.060	1.140	8.900
15	Iowa	12	9	3	1.060	1.330	8.880
16	Kansas State	14	11	3	1.060	1.270	8.840
17	Utah	11	9	2	1.070	1.100	8.790
18	Nebraska	12	9	3	1.060	1.170	8.470
19	Mississippi	12	9	3	1.060	1.140	8.400
20	Southern Mississippi	12	9	3	1.060	1.170	8.240
21	Oklahoma State	12	9	3	1.050	1.130	8.230
22	Bowling Green	13	10	3	1.050	1.210	8.230
23	Washington State	12	9	3	1.060	1.120	8.190
24	Minnesota	12	9	3	1.060	1.110	8.190
25	Florida	12	8	4	1.030	1.240	7.970
26	Maryland	12	9	3	1.050	1.150	7.940
27	Michigan State	12	8	4	1.040	1.140	7.930
28	Northern Illinois	12	10	2	1.070	1.120	7.870
29	Arkansas	12	8	4	1.040	1.210	7.700
30	Pittsburgh	12	8	4	1.040	1.070	7.510
31	Oregon	12	8	4	1.040	1.110	7.490
32	West Virginia	12	8	4	1.040	1.100	7.280
33	Connecticut	12	9	3	1.050	1.050	7.120
34	Louisville	12	9	3	1.060	1.080	7.040
35	Virginia Tech	12	8	4	1.030	1.160	7.000
36	Missouri	12	8	4	1.030	1.080	6.950
37	Clemson	12	8	4	1.030	1.110	6.910
38	Wisconsin	12	7	5	1.020	1.180	6.820
39	Texas Tech	12	7	5	1.020	1.110	6.800
40	North Texas	12	9	3	1.060	1.060	6.620
41	Memphis	12	8	4	1.030	1.070	6.610
42	North Carolina State	12	7	5	1.010	1.110	6.600
43	Marshall	12	8	4	1.030	1.070	6.560
44	Boston College	12	7	5	1.020	1.080	6.500
45	New Mexico	12	8	4	1.030	1.080	6.490
46	Virginia	12	7	5	1.020	1.030	6.430
47	Toledo	12	8	4	1.030	1.120	6.430
48	Colorado State	12	7	5	1.010	0.980	6.380
49	Auburn	12	7	5	1.010	1.130	6.360
50	Oregon State	12	7	5	1.010	1.120	6.330

Weighted Wins Standings for the Year 2004

No.	Team	G	W	L	IW	FW	WW
1	*Southern California*	*12*	*12*	*0*	*1.120*	*1.360*	*11.450*
2	Oklahoma	12	12	0	1.120	1.360	11.330
3	Auburn	12	12	0	1.110	1.360	11.130
4	Utah	11	11	0	1.110	1.170	10.400
5	Texas	11	10	1	1.090	1.230	10.060
6	Boise State	11	11	0	1.110	1.220	10.040
7	California	11	10	1	1.090	1.170	10.020
8	Virginia Tech	12	10	2	1.070	1.190	9.350
9	Iowa	11	9	2	1.070	1.200	9.310
10	Louisville	11	10	1	1.090	1.140	9.300
11	Michigan	11	9	2	1.070	1.200	9.170
12	Louisiana State	11	9	2	1.070	1.130	8.750
13	Wisconsin	11	9	2	1.070	1.110	8.600
14	Tennessee	12	9	3	1.060	1.160	8.580
15	Arizona State	11	8	3	1.050	1.120	8.580
16	Miami-Florida	11	8	3	1.050	1.240	8.420
17	Virginia	11	8	3	1.050	1.080	8.340
18	Florida State	11	8	3	1.050	1.140	8.270
19	Georgia	11	9	2	1.060	1.180	8.260
20	Texas A&M	11	7	4	1.030	1.060	7.670
21	Toledo	12	9	3	1.060	1.140	7.410
22	Ohio State	11	7	4	1.030	1.120	7.370
23	Texas Tech	11	7	4	1.030	1.060	7.340
24	Oklahoma State	11	7	4	1.030	1.060	7.320
25	Purdue	11	7	4	1.030	1.080	7.300
26	Boston College	11	8	3	1.040	1.070	6.900
27	Pittsburgh	11	8	3	1.040	1.110	6.900
28	Oregon State	11	6	5	1.010	1.040	6.640
29	Notre Dame	11	6	5	1.010	1.180	6.610
30	West Virginia	11	8	3	1.040	1.070	6.610
31	New Mexico	11	7	4	1.030	1.030	6.500
32	Florida	11	7	4	1.030	1.040	6.480
33	Bowling Green	11	8	3	1.040	1.050	6.460
34	Miami-Ohio	12	8	4	1.030	1.100	6.420
35	Colorado	12	7	5	1.020	1.040	6.400
36	Texas El-Paso	11	8	3	1.040	1.050	6.370
37	Memphis	11	8	3	1.040	1.050	6.350
38	Clemson	11	6	5	1.010	0.990	6.320
39	Univ Alabama-Birmingham	11	7	4	1.030	1.020	6.260
40	Syracuse	11	6	5	1.010	1.040	6.150
41	UCLA	11	6	5	1.010	1.000	6.150
42	Fresno State	11	8	3	1.040	1.060	5.970
43	Northern Illinois	11	8	3	1.040	1.080	5.930
44	Navy	11	9	2	1.050	1.030	5.930
45	North Carolina	11	6	5	1.000	1.050	5.890
46	Cincinnati	11	6	5	1.010	1.020	5.860
47	South Carolina	11	6	5	1.010	1.000	5.780
48	Georgia Tech	11	6	5	1.000	1.030	5.780
49	Southern Mississippi	11	6	5	1.010	1.030	5.610
50	Arkansas	11	5	6	0.990	0.990	5.560

Weighted Wins Standings for the Year 2005

No.	Team	G	W	L	IW	FW	WW
1	*Texas*	*12*	*12*	*0*	*1.120*	*1.320*	*11.390*
2	Southern California	12	12	0	1.120	1.400	11.240
3	Penn State	11	10	1	1.090	1.290	10.660
4	Virginia Tech	12	10	2	1.080	1.250	9.810
5	Ohio State	11	9	2	1.070	1.210	9.660
6	Miami-Florida	11	9	2	1.070	1.210	9.540
7	Georgia	12	10	2	1.080	1.260	9.500
8	Texas Christian	11	10	1	1.090	1.140	9.270
9	Oregon	11	10	1	1.080	1.150	9.180
10	Notre Dame	11	9	2	1.070	1.120	9.070
11	Louisiana State	12	10	2	1.070	1.250	9.060
12	Alabama	11	9	2	1.070	1.160	9.040
13	West Virginia	11	10	1	1.080	1.170	8.960
14	UCLA	11	9	2	1.070	1.070	8.650
15	Wisconsin	12	9	3	1.060	1.130	8.530
16	Florida	11	8	3	1.050	1.190	8.470
17	Boston College	11	8	3	1.050	1.080	8.440
18	Louisville	11	9	2	1.070	1.090	8.370
19	Auburn	11	9	2	1.060	1.240	8.230
20	Michigan	11	7	4	1.030	1.170	7.950
21	Northwestern	11	7	4	1.030	1.110	7.810
22	Georgia Tech	11	7	4	1.030	1.190	7.790
23	Minnesota	11	7	4	1.030	1.110	7.700
24	Oklahoma	11	7	4	1.030	1.090	7.600
25	South Carolina	11	7	4	1.030	1.120	7.450
26	Clemson	11	7	4	1.030	1.060	7.450
27	Florida State	12	8	4	1.030	1.230	7.450
28	Boise State	12	9	3	1.050	1.120	7.380
29	Texas Tech	11	9	2	1.050	1.060	7.180
30	Nevada	11	8	3	1.050	1.070	6.990
31	Colorado	12	7	5	1.020	1.040	6.930
32	Central Florida	12	8	4	1.040	1.050	6.810
33	Tulsa	12	8	4	1.040	1.090	6.780
34	Fresno State	12	8	4	1.030	1.120	6.750
35	Toledo	11	8	3	1.040	1.070	6.660
36	Virginia	11	6	5	1.010	1.070	6.560
37	Iowa	11	7	4	1.020	1.110	6.520
38	Arizona State	11	6	5	1.010	1.030	6.460
39	Miami-Ohio	11	7	4	1.030	1.050	6.400
40	Louisiana Tech	11	7	4	1.030	1.060	6.270
41	Missouri	11	6	5	1.010	1.040	6.190
42	Central Michigan	11	6	5	1.010	1.040	6.150
43	Nebraska	11	7	4	1.020	1.060	6.140
44	Iowa State	11	7	4	1.020	1.040	6.090
45	North Carolina	11	5	6	0.990	1.050	5.950
46	Navy	11	7	4	1.030	1.010	5.870
47	Maryland	11	5	6	0.990	1.030	5.860
48	California	11	7	4	1.020	1.000	5.780
49	North Carolina State	11	6	5	1.000	1.030	5.770
50	Purdue	11	5	6	0.990	1.010	5.690

Weighted Wins Standings for the Year 2006

No.	Team	G	W	L	IW	FW	WW
1	*Florida*	*13*	*12*	*1*	*1.100*	*1.360*	*11.000*
2	Ohio State	12	12	0	1.120	1.310	10.940
3	Louisville	12	11	1	1.100	1.230	10.470
4	Boise State	12	12	0	1.110	1.290	10.390
5	Michigan	12	11	1	1.100	1.350	10.200
6	Southern California	12	10	2	1.080	1.330	10.150
7	Louisiana State	12	10	2	1.080	1.210	9.690
8	Auburn	12	10	2	1.080	1.270	9.500
9	Notre Dame	12	10	2	1.080	1.240	9.400
10	Wake Forest	13	11	2	1.080	1.200	9.240
11	Oklahoma	13	11	2	1.090	1.220	9.150
12	Virginia Tech	12	10	2	1.070	1.200	9.140
13	Wisconsin	12	11	1	1.090	1.140	9.120
14	West Virginia	12	10	2	1.070	1.190	9.100
15	Rutgers	12	10	2	1.070	1.300	9.010
16	California	12	9	3	1.050	1.120	8.830
17	Arkansas	13	10	3	1.060	1.210	8.760
18	Tennessee	12	9	3	1.060	1.160	8.630
19	Brigham Young	12	10	2	1.080	1.180	8.470
20	Texas	12	9	3	1.050	1.210	8.210
21	Boston College	12	9	3	1.050	1.240	8.160
22	Oregon State	13	9	4	1.040	1.200	8.030
23	Houston	13	10	3	1.060	1.100	7.790
24	Texas A&M	12	9	3	1.050	1.130	7.790
25	Texas Christian	12	10	2	1.070	1.080	7.790
26	Georgia Tech	13	9	4	1.040	1.150	7.600
27	Maryland	12	8	4	1.030	1.070	7.430
28	Hawaii	13	10	3	1.060	1.150	7.400
29	Nebraska	13	9	4	1.040	1.130	7.340
30	Clemson	12	8	4	1.040	1.160	7.260
31	Georgia	12	8	4	1.030	1.110	7.210
32	UCLA	12	7	5	1.020	1.160	7.150
33	Penn State	12	8	4	1.030	1.050	7.130
34	South Carolina	12	7	5	1.010	1.060	7.030
35	Navy	12	9	3	1.050	1.070	7.020
36	Oregon	12	7	5	1.010	1.120	6.830
37	Central Michigan	13	9	4	1.050	1.130	6.770
38	Kentucky	12	7	5	1.010	1.090	6.770
39	South Florida Univ	11	8	3	1.040	1.100	6.770
40	Missouri	12	8	4	1.030	1.040	6.750
41	Arizona State	12	7	5	1.010	1.050	6.600
42	Tulsa	12	8	4	1.030	1.110	6.530
43	Ohio University	13	9	4	1.040	1.050	6.340
44	Arizona	12	6	6	0.990	1.110	6.290
45	Western Michigan	12	8	4	1.040	1.030	6.080
46	Washington State	12	6	6	1.000	1.040	6.060
47	Nevada	12	8	4	1.040	1.030	6.060
48	Southern Mississippi	12	7	5	1.010	1.070	6.020
49	San Jose State	12	8	4	1.030	1.010	6.000
50	Florida State	12	6	6	1.000	1.000	5.970

Weighted Wins Standings for the Year 2007

No.	Team	G	W	L	IW	FW	WW
1	Missouri	13	11	2	1.080	1.260	9.950
2	Ohio State	12	11	1	1.090	1.250	9.900
3	*Louisiana State*	*13*	*11*	*2*	*1.090*	*1.300*	*9.780*
4	Virginia Tech	13	11	2	1.080	1.300	9.740
5	Georgia	12	10	2	1.070	1.190	9.560
6	Kansas	12	11	1	1.090	1.130	9.470
7	Oklahoma	13	11	2	1.090	1.370	9.430
8	West Virginia	12	10	2	1.080	1.180	9.240
9	Arizona State	12	10	2	1.080	1.110	9.160
10	Southern California	12	10	2	1.080	1.150	9.120
11	Florida	12	9	3	1.050	1.180	8.780
12	Brigham Young	12	10	2	1.070	1.210	8.700
13	Hawaii	12	12	0	1.100	1.200	8.690
14	Boston College	13	10	3	1.060	1.260	8.680
15	South Florida Univ	12	9	3	1.050	1.250	8.500
16	Texas	12	9	3	1.060	1.150	8.270
17	Clemson	12	9	3	1.050	1.140	8.260
18	Virginia	12	9	3	1.060	1.110	8.210
19	Illinois	12	9	3	1.050	1.250	8.210
20	Cincinnati	12	9	3	1.050	1.150	8.090
21	Connecticut	12	9	3	1.050	1.110	8.000
22	Central Florida	13	10	3	1.070	1.200	7.930
23	Wisconsin	12	9	3	1.050	1.120	7.840
24	Boise State	12	10	2	1.070	1.070	7.800
25	Tennessee	13	9	4	1.050	1.170	7.790
26	Auburn	12	8	4	1.030	1.100	7.590
27	Air Force	12	9	3	1.050	1.110	7.510
28	Oregon State	12	8	4	1.030	1.110	7.400
29	Penn State	12	8	4	1.040	1.110	7.250
30	Oregon	12	8	4	1.040	1.270	7.240
31	Wake Forest	12	8	4	1.040	1.080	7.230
32	Arkansas	12	8	4	1.030	1.140	7.010
33	Tulsa	13	9	4	1.050	1.100	6.920
34	Utah	12	8	4	1.040	1.010	6.890
35	Texas A&M	12	7	5	1.010	1.080	6.800
36	Texas Tech	12	8	4	1.030	1.120	6.800
37	Michigan	12	8	4	1.040	1.060	6.800
38	Florida State	12	7	5	1.020	1.060	6.780
39	Kentucky	12	7	5	1.010	1.130	6.640
40	Troy State	12	8	4	1.030	1.030	6.450
41	Michigan State	12	7	5	1.020	1.100	6.440
42	Georgia Tech	12	7	5	1.010	1.050	6.410
43	New Mexico	12	8	4	1.030	1.030	6.410
44	Fresno State	12	8	4	1.030	1.030	6.250
45	Rutgers	12	7	5	1.010	1.080	6.250
46	Houston	12	8	4	1.030	1.020	6.070
47	Indiana	12	7	5	1.010	1.020	6.050
48	Oklahoma State	12	6	6	0.990	1.040	6.010
49	East Carolina	12	7	5	1.020	1.040	6.010
50	South Carolina	12	6	6	0.990	1.040	5.940

Weighted Wins Standings for the Year 2008

No.	Team	G	W	L	IW	FW	WW
1	Oklahoma	13	12	1	1.100	1.470	11.040
2	Texas	12	11	1	1.100	1.370	10.740
3	Utah	12	12	0	1.110	1.320	10.570
4	*Florida*	*13*	*12*	*1*	*1.100*	*1.320*	*10.430*
5	Boise State	12	12	0	1.110	1.200	10.270
6	Southern California	12	11	1	1.100	1.290	10.150
7	Penn State	12	11	1	1.090	1.270	10.080
8	Alabama	13	12	1	1.110	1.210	10.060
9	Texas Tech	12	11	1	1.080	1.290	9.470
10	Cincinnati	13	11	2	1.080	1.190	9.300
11	Ohio State	12	10	2	1.070	1.220	9.160
12	Ball State	13	12	1	1.100	1.210	9.050
13	Texas Christian	12	10	2	1.070	1.170	8.840
14	Oklahoma State	12	9	3	1.050	1.110	8.390
15	Georgia	13	10	3	1.060	1.110	8.290
16	Brigham Young	12	10	2	1.070	1.100	8.250
17	Michigan State	12	9	3	1.060	1.150	8.220
18	Pittsburgh	12	9	3	1.060	1.200	8.210
19	Oregon	12	9	3	1.060	1.120	8.120
20	Missouri	13	9	4	1.040	1.120	7.800
21	Virginia Tech	13	9	4	1.040	1.200	7.760
22	Northwestern	12	9	3	1.050	1.020	7.730
23	Boston College	13	9	4	1.040	1.130	7.710
24	North Carolina	12	8	4	1.030	1.100	7.700
25	Nebraska	12	8	4	1.040	1.100	7.590
26	Oregon State	12	8	4	1.040	1.180	7.540
27	Rice	13	10	3	1.070	1.070	7.490
28	Georgia Tech	12	9	3	1.040	1.140	7.460
29	Western Michigan	12	9	3	1.050	1.080	7.450
30	West Virginia	12	8	4	1.030	1.030	7.180
31	California	12	8	4	1.040	1.160	7.160
32	Iowa	12	8	4	1.030	1.110	7.000
33	Florida State	12	8	4	1.020	1.080	6.980
34	Mississippi	12	8	4	1.030	1.140	6.960
35	Tulsa	12	9	3	1.050	1.090	6.950
36	East Carolina	12	8	4	1.040	1.120	6.860
37	Navy	12	8	4	1.030	1.040	6.840
38	Kansas	12	7	5	1.010	1.050	6.810
39	Miami-Florida	12	7	5	1.010	1.060	6.770
40	Central Michigan	12	8	4	1.030	0.980	6.700
41	Air Force	12	8	4	1.030	1.030	6.690
42	Wake Forest	12	7	5	1.020	1.060	6.530
43	Maryland	12	7	5	1.010	1.050	6.520
44	South Florida Univ	12	7	5	1.010	1.000	6.370
45	South Carolina	12	7	5	1.010	1.040	6.360
46	Connecticut	12	7	5	1.010	1.090	6.280
47	Rutgers	12	7	5	1.010	1.090	6.230
48	Wisconsin	12	7	5	1.010	0.980	6.200
49	Louisiana State	12	7	5	1.010	1.010	6.030
50	Minnesota	12	7	5	1.010	0.950	5.830

Weighted Wins Standings for the Year 2009

No.	Team	G	W	L	IW	FW	WW
1	*Alabama*	13	13	0	1.120	1.440	11.950
2	Texas	13	13	0	1.130	1.330	11.150
3	Cincinnati	12	12	0	1.110	1.300	11.050
4	Florida	13	12	1	1.100	1.280	10.940
5	Boise State	13	13	0	1.120	1.310	10.650
6	Texas Christian	12	12	0	1.110	1.280	10.380
7	Oregon	12	10	2	1.080	1.270	9.960
8	Georgia Tech	13	11	2	1.080	1.200	9.360
9	Iowa	12	10	2	1.070	1.220	9.210
10	Ohio State	12	10	2	1.080	1.280	8.880
11	Louisiana State	12	9	3	1.060	1.090	8.720
12	Penn State	12	10	2	1.070	1.160	8.700
13	Virginia Tech	12	9	3	1.060	1.220	8.620
14	Brigham Young	12	10	2	1.080	1.150	8.620
15	Central Michigan	14	12	2	1.090	1.160	8.460
16	Miami-Florida	12	9	3	1.050	1.170	8.310
17	Pittsburgh	12	9	3	1.050	1.070	8.250
18	West Virginia	12	9	3	1.050	1.160	8.220
19	Wisconsin	12	9	3	1.050	1.090	8.110
20	Oklahoma State	12	9	3	1.050	1.110	8.090
21	Arizona	12	8	4	1.030	1.210	7.830
22	Oregon State	12	8	4	1.030	1.100	7.820
23	Southern California	12	8	4	1.040	1.160	7.780
24	Utah	12	9	3	1.060	1.070	7.720
25	Houston	13	10	3	1.060	1.110	7.510
26	Troy State	12	9	3	1.060	1.120	7.500
27	Stanford	12	8	4	1.040	1.130	7.480
28	California	12	8	4	1.030	1.080	7.300
29	Nebraska	13	9	4	1.050	1.080	7.220
30	East Carolina	12	8	4	1.030	1.130	7.010
31	Missouri	12	8	4	1.030	1.040	6.980
32	Central Florida	12	8	4	1.030	1.090	6.930
33	Middle Tennessee	12	9	3	1.060	1.030	6.920
34	Boston College	12	8	4	1.030	1.120	6.890
35	South Carolina	12	7	5	1.010	1.070	6.880
36	Arkansas	12	7	5	1.010	1.100	6.840
37	Tennessee	12	7	5	1.020	1.090	6.820
38	Texas Tech	12	8	4	1.030	1.090	6.770
39	Clemson	13	8	5	1.020	1.070	6.730
40	Fresno State	12	8	4	1.030	1.050	6.680
41	Kentucky	13	8	5	1.020	1.010	6.650
42	Oklahoma	12	7	5	1.010	1.060	6.610
43	Connecticut	12	7	5	1.010	1.050	6.600
44	Mississippi	12	8	4	1.020	1.080	6.590
45	Auburn	11	7	4	1.020	1.110	6.550
46	North Carolina	12	8	4	1.020	1.090	6.500
47	Nevada	12	8	4	1.040	1.020	6.470
48	Navy	12	8	4	1.030	1.020	6.410
49	Northwestern	12	8	4	1.030	1.080	6.410
50	Ohio University	13	9	4	1.040	1.090	6.350

Weighted Wins Standings for the Year 2010

No.	Team	G	W	L	IW	FW	WW
1	*Auburn*	*13*	*13*	*0*	*1.120*	*1.420*	*11.670*
2	Oregon	12	12	0	1.110	1.250	10.360
3	Texas Christian	12	12	0	1.110	1.270	10.280
4	Oklahoma	13	11	2	1.090	1.320	10.020
5	Ohio State	12	11	1	1.100	1.170	9.960
6	Michigan State	12	11	1	1.090	1.230	9.840
7	Stanford	12	11	1	1.090	1.160	9.780
8	Missouri	12	10	2	1.070	1.290	9.640
9	Boise State	12	11	1	1.100	1.320	9.520
10	Nevada	13	12	1	1.100	1.230	9.490
11	Louisiana State	12	10	2	1.070	1.220	9.440
12	Wisconsin	12	11	1	1.090	1.220	9.430
13	Arkansas	12	10	2	1.070	1.260	9.420
14	Oklahoma State	12	10	2	1.080	1.240	9.420
15	Texas A&M	12	9	3	1.050	1.220	8.930
16	Nebraska	13	10	3	1.060	1.200	8.610
17	Utah	12	10	2	1.080	1.150	8.520
18	Virginia Tech	13	11	2	1.090	1.090	8.360
19	Alabama	12	9	3	1.050	1.170	8.320
20	South Carolina	13	9	4	1.040	1.150	8.190
21	West Virginia	12	9	3	1.050	1.100	7.860
22	Hawaii	13	10	3	1.060	1.170	7.680
23	Navy	12	9	3	1.050	1.010	7.570
24	Florida State	13	9	4	1.040	1.100	7.550
25	Tulsa	12	9	3	1.050	1.100	7.450
26	Central Florida	13	10	3	1.060	1.070	7.410
27	Mississippi State	12	8	4	1.030	1.040	7.350
28	North Carolina State	12	8	4	1.030	1.140	7.240
29	Maryland	12	8	4	1.030	1.110	6.890
30	Air Force	12	8	4	1.030	1.080	6.710
31	Texas Tech	12	7	5	1.010	1.050	6.600
32	Notre Dame	12	7	5	1.020	1.150	6.580
33	Michigan	12	7	5	1.010	1.060	6.550
34	Northern Illinois	13	10	3	1.060	1.090	6.540
35	Fresno State	12	8	4	1.030	0.990	6.510
36	Connecticut	12	8	4	1.030	1.040	6.480
37	Florida	12	7	5	1.010	1.060	6.470
38	Southern Mississippi	12	8	4	1.030	1.050	6.430
39	Baylor	12	7	5	1.010	1.020	6.420
40	Penn State	12	7	5	1.010	1.050	6.410
41	San Diego State	12	8	4	1.030	1.060	6.400
42	Boston College	12	7	5	1.010	1.010	6.290
43	Miami-Florida	12	7	5	1.010	1.000	6.230
44	Kansas State	12	7	5	1.010	1.050	6.210
45	Pittsburgh	12	7	5	1.010	1.020	6.180
46	North Carolina	12	7	5	1.010	1.040	6.170
47	Toledo	12	8	4	1.040	1.000	6.150
48	Iowa	12	7	5	1.010	1.060	6.110
49	Southern California	13	8	5	1.030	1.080	6.110
50	Temple	12	8	4	1.030	1.060	6.050

Weighted Wins Standings for the Year 2011

No.	Team	G	W	L	IW	FW	WW
1	Louisiana State	13	13	0	1.120	1.500	11.740
2	Oklahoma State	12	11	1	1.100	1.370	10.750
3	*Alabama*	*12*	*11*	*1*	*1.090*	*1.220*	*10.450*
4	Stanford	12	11	1	1.100	1.240	9.780
5	Houston	13	12	1	1.100	1.180	9.700
6	Kansas State	12	10	2	1.070	1.150	9.690
7	Boise State	12	11	1	1.100	1.280	9.580
8	Virginia Tech	13	11	2	1.080	1.220	9.520
9	Oregon	13	11	2	1.080	1.220	9.390
10	Michigan	12	10	2	1.080	1.210	9.300
11	South Carolina	12	10	2	1.070	1.190	9.270
12	Arkansas	12	10	2	1.070	1.150	9.210
13	Wisconsin	13	11	2	1.080	1.300	9.130
14	Baylor	12	9	3	1.050	1.210	8.990
15	Southern California	12	10	2	1.080	1.220	8.950
16	Oklahoma	12	9	3	1.060	1.200	8.900
17	Georgia	13	10	3	1.060	1.100	8.740
18	Southern Mississippi	13	11	2	1.080	1.190	8.590
19	Texas Christian	12	10	2	1.070	1.250	8.500
20	Michigan State	13	10	3	1.060	1.230	8.480
21	Clemson	13	10	3	1.060	1.270	8.430
22	Penn State	12	9	3	1.050	1.090	8.400
23	Nebraska	12	9	3	1.050	1.170	8.320
24	West Virginia	12	9	3	1.050	1.090	8.320
25	Arkansas State	12	10	2	1.070	1.150	7.870
26	Northern Illinois	13	10	3	1.060	0.970	7.710
27	Notre Dame	12	8	4	1.040	1.070	7.440
28	Tulsa	12	8	4	1.040	1.050	7.390
29	Brigham Young	12	9	3	1.050	1.060	7.120
30	Texas	12	7	5	1.020	1.070	7.010
31	Georgia Tech	12	8	4	1.030	1.090	6.950
32	Missouri	12	7	5	1.010	1.020	6.950
33	Cincinnati	11	8	3	1.040	1.020	6.930
34	Rutgers	12	8	4	1.030	1.060	6.850
35	Toledo	12	8	4	1.030	1.040	6.830
36	Auburn	12	7	5	1.010	1.090	6.830
37	Florida State	12	8	4	1.030	1.020	6.820
38	Virginia	12	8	4	1.030	1.090	6.720
39	North Carolina	12	7	5	1.010	1.070	6.480
40	Louisiana-Lafayette	12	8	4	1.030	1.020	6.300
41	Texas A&M	12	6	6	1.000	1.060	6.290
42	San Diego State	12	8	4	1.030	1.030	6.240
43	Iowa	12	7	5	1.010	1.020	6.210
44	Louisiana Tech	12	8	4	1.030	1.030	6.190
45	Washington	12	7	5	1.010	0.980	6.180
46	Louisville	12	7	5	1.010	1.080	6.110
47	Iowa State	12	6	6	0.990	1.100	6.100
48	Temple	12	8	4	1.030	1.040	6.060
49	California	12	7	5	1.010	1.010	5.980
50	Florida International	12	8	4	1.040	0.990	5.960

Weighted Wins Standings for the Year 2012

No.	Team	G	W	L	IW	FW	WW
1	Notre Dame	12	12	0	1.120	1.390	11.680
2	OHIO ST.—not eligible	12	12	0	1.120	1.330	11.320
3	Florida	12	11	1	1.090	1.450	11.020
4	*Alabama*	*13*	*12*	*1*	*1.100*	*1.330*	*10.630*
5	Oregon	12	11	1	1.090	1.290	10.450
6	Kansas State	12	11	1	1.090	1.250	10.370
7	Stanford	13	11	2	1.090	1.420	10.250
8	Louisiana State	12	10	2	1.070	1.240	9.920
9	Oklahoma	12	10	2	1.070	1.160	9.790
10	Georgia	13	11	2	1.080	1.200	9.650
11	South Carolina	12	10	2	1.070	1.280	9.590
12	Nebraska	13	10	3	1.060	1.270	8.960
13	Texas A&M	12	10	2	1.060	1.250	8.920
14	Northern Illinois	13	12	1	1.100	1.240	8.890
15	Clemson	12	10	2	1.070	1.140	8.860
16	Florida State	13	11	2	1.070	1.150	8.840
17	San Jose State	12	10	2	1.070	1.220	8.730
18	Kent State	13	11	2	1.080	1.160	8.340
19	Louisville	12	10	2	1.070	1.170	8.150
20	Oregon State	12	9	3	1.040	1.140	8.010
21	Boise State	12	10	2	1.080	1.150	7.990
22	Utah State	12	10	2	1.070	1.200	7.980
23	Northwestern	12	9	3	1.050	1.100	7.940
24	UCLA	13	9	4	1.050	1.080	7.920
25	Michigan	12	8	4	1.040	1.090	7.900
26	Arkansas State	13	10	3	1.060	1.170	7.840
27	Ball State	12	9	3	1.060	1.140	7.710
28	Texas	12	8	4	1.040	1.070	7.440
29	Penn State	12	8	4	1.040	1.090	7.430
30	Tulsa	13	10	3	1.060	1.130	7.420
31	Rutgers	12	9	3	1.050	1.100	7.370
32	Louisiana Tech	12	9	3	1.060	1.060	7.320
33	Vanderbilt	12	8	4	1.030	1.030	7.320
34	Fresno State	11	8	3	1.050	1.110	7.310
35	Toledo	12	9	3	1.050	1.120	7.290
36	Southern California	12	7	5	1.020	1.060	7.120
37	San Diego State	12	9	3	1.050	1.140	7.080
38	Wisconsin	13	8	5	1.020	1.150	7.030
39	Mississippi State	12	8	4	1.030	1.060	7.030
40	Arizona	12	7	5	1.010	1.100	6.950
41	Cincinnati	12	9	3	1.040	1.060	6.880
42	Oklahoma State	12	7	5	1.010	1.070	6.810
43	Washington	12	7	5	1.010	1.130	6.750
44	Navy	12	8	4	1.030	1.040	6.630
45	Central Florida	13	9	4	1.050	1.040	6.620
46	Louisiana-Lafayette	12	8	4	1.030	1.030	6.600
47	Baylor	12	7	5	1.010	1.150	6.590
48	Texas Christian	12	7	5	1.010	1.060	6.550
49	Louisiana-Monroe	12	8	4	1.040	1.020	6.430
50	North Carolina	12	8	4	1.030	1.020	6.410

Weighted Wins Standings for the Year 2013

No.	Team	G	W	L	IW	FW	WW
1	*Florida State*	*13*	*13*	*0*	*1.120*	*1.310*	*11.000*
2	Auburn	13	12	1	1.100	1.330	10.990
3	Ohio State	13	12	1	1.100	1.270	10.370
4	Michigan State	13	12	1	1.100	1.310	10.360
5	Stanford	13	11	2	1.090	1.390	10.320
6	Missouri	13	11	2	1.080	1.190	9.920
7	Baylor	12	11	1	1.090	1.270	9.840
8	Arizona State	13	10	3	1.060	1.260	9.620
9	Alabama	12	11	1	1.080	1.200	9.530
10	South Carolina	12	10	2	1.070	1.310	9.350
11	Oregon	12	10	2	1.070	1.160	9.320
12	Central Florida	12	11	1	1.100	1.240	9.260
13	Oklahoma	12	10	2	1.080	1.220	9.170
14	Fresno State	12	11	1	1.090	1.150	9.120
15	Northern Illinois	13	12	1	1.100	1.210	9.080
16	Oklahoma State	12	10	2	1.070	1.190	8.970
17	UCLA	12	9	3	1.060	1.180	8.790
18	Louisville	12	11	1	1.090	1.180	8.460
19	Clemson	12	10	2	1.060	1.110	8.450
20	Louisiana State	12	9	3	1.050	1.180	8.240
21	Duke	13	10	3	1.060	1.160	8.230
22	Miami-Florida	12	9	3	1.050	1.050	8.150
23	Wisconsin	12	9	3	1.050	1.140	8.130
24	Southern California	13	9	4	1.050	1.160	8.050
25	Georgia	12	8	4	1.030	1.190	8.050
26	Notre Dame	12	8	4	1.040	1.300	8.020
27	Rice	13	10	3	1.070	1.140	7.780
28	Brigham Young	12	8	4	1.030	1.060	7.720
29	Texas A&M	12	8	4	1.030	1.140	7.710
30	Ball State	12	10	2	1.070	1.080	7.690
31	Washington	12	8	4	1.030	1.070	7.630
32	Virginia Tech	12	8	4	1.030	1.170	7.580
33	Bowling Green	12	9	3	1.060	1.160	7.530
34	Minnesota	12	8	4	1.030	1.090	7.510
35	Iowa	12	8	4	1.030	1.110	7.250
36	Texas	12	8	4	1.040	1.150	7.040
37	Michigan	12	7	5	1.020	1.090	7.040
38	Vanderbilt	12	8	4	1.030	1.060	6.920
39	Mississippi	12	7	5	1.010	1.120	6.770
40	Arizona	12	7	5	1.010	1.100	6.730
41	Navy	12	8	4	1.030	1.030	6.620
42	Penn State	12	7	5	1.020	1.060	6.510
43	Houston	11	7	4	1.030	1.120	6.500
44	North Texas	12	8	4	1.040	1.210	6.450
45	East Carolina	12	9	3	1.050	1.080	6.410
46	Mississippi State	12	6	6	0.990	1.060	6.380
47	Nebraska	12	8	4	1.030	1.070	6.380
48	Marshall	13	9	4	1.040	1.110	6.190
49	Cincinnati	12	9	3	1.050	0.950	6.160
50	Univ of Texas at San Ant	12	7	5	1.020	1.070	6.140

Pre-Bowl Championship Series (Pre-BCS) Era

1981–1997

Weighted Wins Standings for the Year 1981

No.	Team	G	W	L	T	IW	FW	WW
1	*Clemson*	11	11	0	0	1.100	1.280	9.740
2	Georgia	11	10	1	0	1.090	1.140	8.850
3	Pittsburgh	11	10	1	0	1.090	1.170	8.807
4	Texas	11	9	1	1	1.085	1.272	8.734
5	Alabama	11	9	1	1	1.085	1.147	8.489
6	Penn State	11	9	2	0	1.070	1.280	8.403
7	Southern California	11	9	2	0	1.070	1.225	8.310
8	Miami-Florida	10	8	2	0	1.060	1.205	8.290
9	Michigan	10	8	2	0	1.060	1.115	8.045
10	Arizona State	11	9	2	0	1.060	1.235	8.040
11	Southern Methodist	11	10	1	0	1.070	1.175	7.760
12	North Carolina	11	9	2	0	1.070	1.135	7.758
13	Nebraska	11	9	2	0	1.070	1.205	7.747
14	Brigham Young	12	10	2	0	1.080	1.205	7.702
15	Hawaii	11	9	2	0	1.060	1.110	7.597
16	Washington State	11	8	2	1	1.055	1.137	7.551
17	Iowa	11	8	3	0	1.050	1.240	7.495
18	UCLA	11	7	3	1	1.045	1.182	7.269
19	Utah	11	8	2	1	1.055	1.105	7.199
20	Washington	11	9	2	0	1.060	1.185	6.965
21	Arkansas	11	8	3	0	1.050	1.095	6.910
22	Wyoming	11	8	3	0	1.040	1.130	6.828
23	San Jose State	11	9	2	0	1.060	1.060	6.760
24	Kansas	11	8	3	0	1.050	1.080	6.652
25	Miami-Ohio	11	8	2	1	1.055	1.087	6.636
26	Illinois	11	7	4	0	1.030	1.100	6.590
27	West Virginia	11	8	3	0	1.050	1.040	6.520
28	Houston	11	7	3	1	1.045	1.137	6.514
29	Wisconsin	10	6	4	0	1.020	1.080	6.373
30	Toledo	11	8	3	0	1.050	1.085	6.205
31	Ohio State	11	8	3	0	1.050	1.150	6.145
32	Oklahoma	11	6	4	1	1.025	1.145	6.136
33	Missouri	11	7	4	0	1.030	1.080	6.120
34	Mississippi State	11	7	4	0	1.030	1.095	6.105
35	Tennessee	12	8	4	0	1.030	0.980	5.952
36	Oklahoma State	11	7	4	0	1.030	1.060	5.893
37	Minnesota	11	6	5	0	1.010	1.050	5.305
38	San Diego State	11	6	5	0	1.010	1.010	5.205
39	Texas A&M	11	6	5	0	1.010	1.025	5.105
40	Florida	11	7	4	0	1.020	1.010	5.070
41	Duke	11	6	5	0	1.010	0.990	4.995
42	Tulane	11	6	5	0	1.010	0.965	4.762
43	Michigan State	11	5	6	0	0.990	1.005	4.742
44	Arizona	11	6	5	0	1.000	0.990	4.730
45	Purdue	11	5	6	0	0.990	0.970	4.730
46	South Carolina	12	6	6	0	1.000	1.065	4.680
47	Florida State	11	6	5	0	1.000	0.050	4.402
48	Boston College	11	5	6	0	0.980	0.970	4.338
49	Syracuse	11	5	6	0	0.980	1.000	4.335
50	Auburn	11	5	6	0	0.990	0.970	4.317

Weighted Wins Standings for the Year 1982

No.	Team	G	W	L	T	IW	FW	WW
1	Georgia	11	11	0	0	1.110	1.365	10.572
2	*Penn State*	*11*	*10*	*1*	*0*	*1.090*	*1.430*	*9.867*
3	Nebraska	12	11	1	0	1.100	1.255	9.557
4	UCLA	11	9	1	1	1.085	1.248	9.121
5	Southern Methodist	11	10	0	1	1.105	1.208	8.961
6	Clemson	11	9	1	1	1.075	1.177	8.506
7	Pittsburgh	11	9	2	0	1.070	1.230	8.500
8	Arizona State	11	9	2	0	1.070	1.155	8.350
9	West Virginia	11	9	2	0	1.060	1.195	8.343
10	Washington	11	9	2	0	1.070	1.245	8.277
11	New Mexico	11	10	1	0	1.090	1.130	8.220
12	Texas	11	9	2	0	1.070	1.155	8.022
13	Southern California	11	8	3	0	1.050	1.180	7.958
14	Florida	11	8	3	0	1.040	1.210	7.890
15	Auburn	11	8	3	0	1.050	1.140	7.835
16	Oklahoma	11	8	3	0	1.050	1.145	7.463
17	Vanderbilt	11	8	3	0	1.040	1.110	7.430
18	Maryland	11	8	3	0	1.040	1.110	7.393
19	Florida State	11	8	3	0	1.040	1.150	7.325
20	Arkansas	11	8	2	1	1.065	1.143	7.324
21	Louisiana State	11	8	3	0	1.050	1.120	7.095
22	Michigan	11	8	3	0	1.050	1.120	7.062
23	Brigham Young	11	8	3	0	1.050	1.130	6.840
24	Ohio State	11	8	3	0	1.050	1.120	6.830
25	Alabama	11	7	4	0	1.030	1.160	6.820
26	Bowling Green	10	7	3	0	1.040	1.105	6.748
27	Western Michigan	11	7	2	2	1.050	1.078	6.685
28	California	11	7	4	0	1.030	1.090	6.625
29	Boston College	11	8	2	1	1.045	1.083	6.439
30	North Carolina	11	7	4	0	1.030	1.110	6.433
31	Notre Dame	11	6	4	1	1.025	1.175	6.381
32	Miami-Florida	11	7	4	0	1.030	1.030	6.350
33	Tennessee	11	7	4	0	1.030	1.110	6.270
34	Southern Mississippi	11	7	4	0	1.030	1.040	6.150
35	Arizona	11	6	4	1	1.025	1.107	6.116
36	San Jose State	11	8	3	0	1.040	1.040	6.047
37	Iowa	11	7	4	0	1.030	1.020	5.998
38	Illinois	11	7	4	0	1.030	1.040	5.840
39	Toledo	10	6	4	0	1.020	1.060	5.712
40	Miami-Ohio	11	7	4	0	1.020	1.085	5.688
41	San Diego State	12	7	5	0	1.020	1.030	5.415
42	North Carolina State	11	6	5	0	1.000	1.010	5.403
43	Georgia Tech	11	6	5	0	1.000	1.030	5.365
44	Central Michigan	11	6	4	1	1.015	1.040	5.219
45	Missouri	11	5	4	2	1.020	1.022	5.190
46	Air Force	12	7	5	0	1.020	1.055	5.135
47	Duke	11	6	5	0	1.010	1.050	5.077
48	Stanford	11	5	6	0	0.990	1.110	5.065
49	Mississippi State	11	5	6	0	0.990	1.040	4.985
50	Wisconsin	11	6	5	0	1.010	1.050	4.878

Weighted Wins Standings for the Year 1983

No.	Team	G	W	L	T	IW	FW	WW
1	Texas	11	11	0	0	1.100	1.355	10.127
2	Auburn	11	10	1	0	1.090	1.405	10.102
3	Nebraska	11	11	0	0	1.110	1.235	10.062
4	Illinois	11	10	1	0	1.090	1.310	9.205
5	*Miami-Florida*	*11*	*10*	*1*	*0*	*1.090*	*1.180*	*9.122*
6	Georgia	11	9	1	1	1.085	1.247	9.066
7	Brigham Young	11	10	1	0	1.090	1.235	8.880
8	Michigan	11	9	2	0	1.070	1.240	8.450
9	Iowa	11	9	2	0	1.070	1.175	8.267
10	Florida	11	8	2	1	1.065	1.210	8.211
11	Clemson	11	9	1	1	1.075	1.208	8.024
12	Northern Illinois	11	9	2	0	1.070	1.170	7.785
13	Pittsburgh	11	8	2	1	1.065	1.147	7.761
14	Southern Methodist	11	10	1	0	1.070	1.125	7.707
15	Maryland	11	8	3	0	1.050	1.165	7.505
16	Air Force	11	9	2	0	1.070	1.085	7.457
17	West Virginia	11	8	3	0	1.050	1.245	7.385
18	Ohio State	11	8	3	0	1.050	1.120	7.125
19	Bowling Green	11	8	3	0	1.050	1.090	6.965
20	Tennessee	11	8	3	0	1.040	1.095	6.942
21	Washington	11	8	3	0	1.050	1.135	6.772
22	Wisconsin	11	7	4	0	1.030	1.130	6.675
23	Alabama	11	7	4	0	1.030	1.070	6.602
24	Oklahoma	12	8	4	0	1.040	1.075	6.495
25	Central Michigan	11	8	3	0	1.040	1.130	6.455
26	Toledo	11	9	2	0	1.050	1.100	6.440
27	Missouri	11	7	4	0	1.030	1.165	6.425
28	Baylor	11	7	3	1	1.045	1.110	6.401
29	North Carolina	11	8	3	0	1.040	1.050	6.322
30	Penn State	12	7	4	1	1.025	1.132	6.291
31	Kentucky	11	6	4	1	1.025	1.065	6.094
32	Oklahoma State	11	7	4	0	1.020	0.980	5.955
33	UCLA	11	6	4	1	1.025	1.052	5.884
34	Boston College	11	9	2	0	1.040	1.170	5.855
35	Florida State	11	6	5	0	1.010	1.025	5.692
36	Syracuse	11	6	5	0	1.010	1.060	5.540
37	Virginia Tech	11	9	2	0	1.040	1.010	5.395
38	Arizona	11	7	3	1	1.045	1.022	5.324
39	Washington State	11	7	4	0	1.020	1.105	5.307
40	Arkansas	11	6	5	0	1.010	1.015	5.197
41	Notre Dame	11	6	5	0	1.010	0.995	5.192
42	Mississippi	11	6	5	0	1.010	1.030	5.118
43	East Carolina	11	8	3	0	1.020	1.060	4.915
44	Southern Mississippi	11	7	4	0	1.010	1.010	4.885
45	Arizona State	11	6	4	1	1.025	1.037	4.839
46	Wyoming	12	7	5	0	1.000	1.015	4.807
47	Memphis	11	6	4	1	1.020	1.030	4.793
48	Texas A&M	11	5	5	1	0.995	0.992	4.417
49	South Carolina	11	5	6	0	0.990	0.960	4.287
50	Michigan State	11	4	6	1	0.985	0.935	4.183

Weighted Wins Standings for the Year 1984

No.	Team	G	W	L	T	IW	FW	WW
1	*Brigham Young*	12	12	0	0	*1.120*	*1.185*	*9.578*
2	Florida	11	9	1	1	1.085	1.317	9.231
3	Washington	11	10	1	0	1.090	1.180	9.125
4	South Carolina	11	10	1	0	1.080	1.160	8.735
5	Oklahoma	11	9	1	1	1.085	1.228	8.726
6	Ohio State	11	9	2	0	1.070	1.175	8.305
7	Nebraska	11	9	2	0	1.070	1.190	7.933
8	Southern Methodist	11	9	2	0	1.060	1.215	7.888
9	Louisiana State	11	8	2	1	1.065	1.198	7.876
10	Oklahoma State	11	9	2	0	1.070	1.110	7.840
11	Boston College	11	9	2	0	1.050	1.140	7.648
12	Maryland	11	8	3	0	1.050	1.185	7.530
13	Southern California	11	8	3	0	1.050	1.190	7.457
14	Texas	11	7	3	1	1.045	1.262	7.194
15	Kentucky	11	8	3	0	1.040	1.115	7.092
16	Tennessee	11	7	3	1	1.045	1.077	7.064
17	Notre Dame	11	7	4	0	1.030	1.165	7.058
18	Texas Christian	11	8	3	0	1.040	1.115	7.052
19	Virginia	11	7	2	2	1.050	1.110	7.045
20	Arkansas	11	7	3	1	1.045	1.075	6.954
21	Miami-Florida	12	8	4	0	1.040	1.225	6.937
22	Auburn	12	8	4	0	1.040	1.155	6.920
23	Purdue	11	7	4	0	1.030	1.160	6.895
24	UCLA	11	8	3	0	1.050	1.100	6.878
25	Florida State	11	7	3	1	1.035	1.075	6.834
26	Georgia	11	7	4	0	1.030	1.090	6.747
27	Illinois	11	7	4	0	1.030	1.105	6.570
28	Wisconsin	10	6	3	1	1.035	1.122	6.516
29	West Virginia	11	7	4	0	1.030	1.110	6.508
30	Toledo	11	8	2	1	1.055	1.110	6.374
31	Michigan State	10	6	4	0	1.020	1.065	6.228
32	Penn State	11	6	5	0	1.000	1.130	6.200
33	Clemson	11	7	4	0	1.020	1.095	6.185
34	Houston	11	7	4	0	1.030	1.055	6.183
35	Syracuse	11	6	5	0	1.010	1.135	6.170
36	Iowa	12	7	4	1	1.035	1.122	6.146
37	Michigan	11	6	5	0	1.010	1.115	6.025
38	Bowling Green	11	8	3	0	1.040	1.040	6.000
39	Rutgers	10	7	3	0	1.030	1.075	5.928
40	Air Force	10	7	3	0	1.030	1.060	5.765
41	Hawaii	11	7	4	0	1.030	1.055	5.645
42	Georgia Tech	11	6	4	1	1.015	1.040	5.612
43	UNLV	12	10	2	0	1.070	1.150	5.468
44	Central Michigan	10	7	2	1	1.045	1.050	5.459
45	Washington State	11	6	5	0	1.010	1.025	5.457
46	Arizona	11	7	4	0	1.030	1.020	5.067
47	Texas A&M	11	6	5	0	1.000	1.035	5.032
48	Virginia Tech	11	8	3	0	1.020	1.020	5.000
49	Baylor	11	5	6	0	0.990	1.035	4.965
50	North Carolina	11	5	5	1	1.005	0.990	4.927

Weighted Wins Standings for the Year 1985

No.	Team	G	W	L	T	IW	FW	WW
1	Penn State	11	11	0	0	1.110	1.305	9.960
2	Miami-Florida	11	10	1	0	1.090	1.270	9.425
3	Florida	11	9	1	1	1.085	1.430	9.301
4	*Oklahoma*	*11*	*10*	*1*	*0*	*1.090*	*1.290*	*9.280*
5	Iowa	11	10	1	0	1.080	1.210	9.080
6	Michigan	11	9	1	1	1.085	1.223	8.994
7	Bowling Green	11	11	0	0	1.100	1.205	8.738
8	Tennessee	11	8	1	2	1.080	1.250	8.675
9	Louisiana State	11	9	1	1	1.085	1.117	8.584
10	Air Force	12	11	1	0	1.100	1.140	8.410
11	Alabama	11	8	2	1	1.065	1.272	8.356
12	Texas A&M	11	9	2	0	1.060	1.190	8.143
13	Auburn	11	8	3	0	1.050	1.190	7.952
14	Nebraska	11	9	2	0	1.070	1.155	7.938
15	Arkansas	11	9	2	0	1.070	1.130	7.875
16	UCLA	11	8	2	1	1.065	1.295	7.600
17	Brigham Young	13	11	2	0	1.090	1.140	7.575
18	Florida State	11	8	3	0	1.040	1.110	7.355
19	Ohio State	11	8	3	0	1.050	1.155	7.333
20	Maryland	11	8	3	0	1.050	1.105	7.330
21	Georgia	11	7	3	1	1.045	1.190	7.289
22	Baylor	11	8	3	0	1.050	1.130	7.240
23	Texas	11	8	3	0	1.050	1.170	7.205
24	Arizona	11	8	3	0	1.050	1.080	6.860
25	Miami-Ohio	11	8	2	1	1.065	1.105	6.689
26	Oklahoma State	11	8	3	0	1.040	1.135	6.495
27	Michigan State	11	7	4	0	1.030	1.070	6.433
28	Georgia Tech	11	8	2	1	1.045	1.140	6.315
29	Colorado	11	7	4	0	1.030	1.080	6.160
30	West Virginia	11	7	3	1	1.045	1.077	6.151
31	Arizona State	11	8	3	0	1.050	1.100	6.135
32	Illinois	11	6	4	1	1.015	1.127	6.016
33	Southern Methodist	11	6	5	0	1.010	1.060	5.490
34	Southern California	11	6	5	0	1.010	1.050	5.393
35	Washington	11	6	5	0	1.010	0.985	5.325
36	Minnesota	11	6	5	0	1.000	1.000	5.323
37	Syracuse	11	7	4	0	1.030	1.015	5.207
38	Notre Dame	11	5	6	0	0.990	1.030	5.165
39	Clemson	11	6	5	0	1.010	0.970	4.860
40	Central Michigan	10	7	3	0	1.040	1.010	4.847
41	Kentucky	11	5	6	0	0.980	0.945	4.785
42	Mississippi State	11	5	6	0	0.980	0.975	4.655
43	Purdue	11	5	6	0	0.990	1.005	4.642
44	Utah	12	8	4	0	1.030	1.010	4.620
45	Fresno State	11	10	0	1	1.095	1.095	4.429
46	Virginia	11	6	5	0	1.000	1.000	4.407
47	Wisconsin	11	5	6	0	0.990	0.990	4.405
48	Pittsburgh	11	5	5	1	1.005	0.937	4.311
49	Southern Mississippi	11	7	4	0	1.010	0.970	4.177
50	Mississippi	11	4	6	1	0.975	0.965	4.117

Weighted Wins Standings for the Year 1986

No.	Team	G	W	L	T	IW	FW	WW
1	*Penn State*	*11*	*11*	*0*	*0*	*1.110*	*1.225*	*10.230*
2	Miami-Florida	11	11	0	0	1.110	1.290	10.212
3	Arizona State	11	9	1	1	1.085	1.235	9.076
4	Oklahoma	11	10	1	0	1.090	1.235	8.907
5	Louisiana State	11	9	2	0	1.070	1.270	8.750
6	Michigan	12	11	1	0	1.100	1.265	8.192
7	Southern California	10	7	3	0	1.040	1.225	7.920
8	Nebraska	11	9	2	0	1.070	1.095	7.820
9	Alabama	12	9	3	0	1.060	1.130	7.805
10	Arkansas	11	9	2	0	1.070	1.190	7.795
11	Stanford	11	8	3	0	1.050	1.185	7.738
12	Arizona	11	8	3	0	1.050	1.145	7.565
13	UCLA	11	7	3	1	1.045	1.212	7.514
14	Georgia	11	8	3	0	1.040	1.135	7.293
15	Washington	12	8	3	1	1.055	1.192	7.226
16	San Diego State	11	8	3	0	1.050	1.120	7.097
17	Baylor	11	8	3	0	1.040	1.160	7.075
18	Ohio State	12	9	3	0	1.060	1.150	7.047
19	Texas A&M	10	8	2	0	1.050	1.130	7.040
20	Auburn	11	9	2	0	1.050	1.120	6.960
21	Clemson	11	7	2	2	1.050	1.137	6.851
22	Boston College	11	8	3	0	1.040	1.045	6.742
23	Texas Tech	10	7	3	0	1.040	1.110	6.700
24	Miami-Ohio	11	8	3	0	1.050	1.080	6.595
25	North Carolina	12	8	3	1	1.045	1.112	6.526
26	Iowa	11	8	3	0	1.050	1.040	6.385
27	Virginia Tech	11	8	2	1	1.045	1.070	6.094
28	Florida	11	6	5	0	1.000	1.120	6.047
29	Mississippi	11	7	3	1	1.040	1.115	6.008
30	Florida State	11	6	4	1	1.025	1.077	5.974
31	Brigham Young	12	8	4	0	1.040	1.030	5.903
32	North Carolina State	10	7	2	1	1.045	1.037	5.866
33	Toledo	11	7	4	0	1.030	1.020	5.427
34	San Jose State	11	9	2	0	1.070	1.110	5.312
35	Oregon	11	5	6	0	0.990	1.070	5.235
36	Mississippi State	11	6	5	0	1.000	1.010	5.215
37	Colorado	11	6	5	0	1.010	1.070	5.195
38	Kentucky	11	5	5	1	1.005	1.007	5.189
39	Notre Dame	11	5	6	0	0.990	1.050	5.168
40	Minnesota	10	6	4	0	1.020	0.130	5.120
41	Michigan State	10	5	5	0	1.000	0.960	5.110
42	Colorado State	11	6	5	0	1.000	0.940	5.065
43	Hawaii	12	7	5	0	1.020	1.080	5.045
44	Pittsburgh	11	5	5	1	1.005	1.012	4.976
45	Wyoming	13	7	6	0	1.010	1.020	4.810
46	Tennessee	11	6	5	0	1.010	1.035	4.748
47	Iowa State	11	6	5	0	1.000	1.010	4.730
48	Rutgers	11	5	5	1	1.005	1.007	4.721
49	Air Force	11	6	5	0	1.010	1.020	4.590
50	Cincinnati	11	5	6	0	0.980	0.995	4.540

Weighted Wins Standings for the Year 1987

No.	Team	G	W	L	T	IW	FW	WW
1	*Miami-Florida*	11	11	0	0	1.110	1.340	10.395
2	Oklahoma	11	11	0	0	1.100	1.300	9.760
3	Syracuse	11	11	0	0	1.100	1.220	9.740
4	Florida State	11	10	1	0	1.080	1.295	9.477
5	Nebraska	11	10	1	0	1.090	1.315	9.363
6	Auburn	11	9	1	1	1.085	1.223	8.919
7	Louisiana State	11	9	1	1	1.085	1.248	8.739
8	UCLA	11	9	2	0	1.070	1.145	8.507
9	Notre Dame	11	8	3	0	1.050	1.295	8.420
10	Michigan State	12	9	2	1	1.075	1.280	8.339
11	Texas A&M	11	9	2	0	1.060	1.155	8.127
12	Oklahoma State	11	9	2	0	1.070	1.180	8.073
13	Wyoming	12	10	2	0	1.080	1.185	7.973
14	Southern California	11	8	3	0	1.050	1.160	7.895
15	Penn State	11	8	3	0	1.050	1.120	7.595
16	Tennessee	12	9	2	1	1.075	1.157	7.579
17	Clemson	11	9	2	0	1.060	1.110	7.570
18	Pittsburgh	11	8	3	0	1.050	1.200	7.455
19	Georgia	11	8	3	0	1.050	1.110	7.390
20	Iowa	11	8	3	0	1.050	1.140	7.125
21	Brigham Young	12	9	3	0	1.060	1.130	7.115
22	Indiana	11	8	3	0	1.050	1.095	7.100
23	Arkansas	12	9	3	0	1.060	1.075	7.053
24	Air Force	12	9	3	0	1.060	1.080	6.810
25	Alabama	11	7	4	0	1.030	1.240	6.723
26	South Carolina	11	8	3	0	1.030	1.120	6.510
27	Michigan	11	7	4	0	1.030	1.080	6.415
28	Eastern Michigan	11	9	2	0	1.060	1.035	6.405
29	Colorado	11	7	4	0	1.030	1.030	6.295
30	Florida	11	6	5	0	1.010	1.040	6.085
31	Washington	11	6	4	1	1.025	1.057	5.995
32	Arizona State	11	6	4	1	1.025	1.042	5.980
33	Ohio State	11	6	4	1	1.025	1.067	5.914
34	Texas	11	6	5	0	1.010	1.060	5.865
35	Tulane	11	7	4	0	1.030	1.030	5.803
36	Virginia	11	7	4	0	1.020	1.000	5.720
37	Oregon	11	6	5	0	1.010	1.085	5.515
38	Texas Tech	11	6	4	1	1.015	1.065	5.511
39	West Virginia	11	6	5	0	1.010	0.990	5.228
40	Boston College	11	5	6	0	0.990	1.115	5.078
41	Rutgers	11	6	5	0	1.010	0.980	5.050
42	Kent State	11	7	4	0	1.030	0.990	4.995
43	Minnesota	11	6	5	0	1.000	0.965	4.917
44	Arizona	11	4	4	3	1.015	1.005	4.891
45	Missouri	11	5	6	0	0.990	0.990	4.740
46	Stanford	11	5	6	0	0.990	1.000	4.615
47	Texas Christian	11	5	6	0	0.980	1.030	4.592
48	San Jose State	11	10	1	0	1.080	1.010	4.552
49	Texas El-Paso	11	7	4	0	1.020	1.020	4.547
50	Wake Forest	11	7	4	0	1.010	0.980	4.530

Weighted Wins Standings for the Year 1988

No.	Team	G	W	L	T	IW	FW	WW
1	*Notre Dame*	11	11	0	0	1.110	1.380	10.498
2	Southern California	11	10	1	0	1.090	1.255	9.998
3	Miami-Florida	11	10	1	0	1.090	1.415	9.820
4	West Virginia	11	11	0	0	1.110	1.180	9.475
5	Nebraska	12	11	1	0	1.100	1.310	9.468
6	Florida State	11	10	1	0	1.080	1.255	9.243
7	Auburn	12	11	1	0	1.100	1.250	8.935
8	Arkansas	11	10	1	0	1.090	1.180	8.905
9	Wyoming	11	10	1	0	1.090	1.300	8.865
10	Oklahoma	11	9	2	0	1.070	1.210	8.368
11	Michigan	11	8	2	1	1.065	1.182	8.362
12	Clemson	11	9	2	0	1.060	1.145	8.150
13	Oklahoma State	11	9	2	0	1.070	1.140	7.953
14	Houston	11	9	2	0	1.070	1.160	7.808
15	Louisiana State	11	8	3	0	1.050	1.185	7.673
16	Syracuse	11	9	2	0	1.070	1.055	7.627
17	Southern Mississippi	11	9	2	0	1.060	1.110	7.575
18	UCLA	10	8	2	0	1.060	1.195	7.470
19	Washington State	11	8	3	0	1.050	1.150	7.407
20	Colorado	11	8	3	0	1.050	1.145	7.178
21	Hawaii	12	9	3	0	1.060	1.105	6.980
22	Alabama	11	8	3	0	1.050	1.050	6.965
23	Arizona	10	6	4	0	1.020	1.105	6.835
24	Louisville	12	9	3	0	1.050	1.050	6.790
25	Texas El-Paso	12	10	2	0	1.060	1.120	6.775
26	Georgia	11	8	3	0	1.040	1.020	6.585
27	Indiana	11	7	3	1	1.045	1.090	6.574
28	Brigham Young	12	8	4	0	1.040	1.110	6.365
29	Duke	11	7	3	1	1.035	1.052	6.286
30	Michigan State	11	6	4	1	1.025	1.097	6.285
31	Virginia	11	7	4	0	1.020	1.045	6.040
32	Illinois	11	6	4	1	1.025	1.070	5.861
33	Arizona State	11	6	5	0	1.000	1.065	5.792
34	South Carolina	11	8	3	0	1.030	1.035	5.772
35	Western Michigan	11	8	3	0	1.050	1.005	5.752
36	Washington	11	6	5	0	1.010	1.045	5.662
37	Ball State	11	8	3	0	1.030	1.055	5.627
38	Texas A&M	12	7	5	0	1.020	1.090	5.605
39	Iowa	12	6	3	3	1.045	1.090	5.551
40	Central Michigan	11	7	4	0	1.020	1.025	5.497
41	North Carolina State	10	7	2	1	1.035	1.112	5.406
42	Eastern Michigan	10	6	3	1	1.025	1.065	5.269
43	Pittsburgh	11	6	5	0	1.000	0.950	5.260
44	Utah	11	6	5	0	1.000	1.020	4.990
45	California	11	5	5	1	1.005	1.010	4.771
46	Stanford	10	3	5	2	0.990	0.992	4.770
47	Oregon	11	6	5	0	1.000	1.045	4.737
48	Florida	12	6	6	0	0.980	0.980	4.720
49	Toledo	10	6	4	0	1.010	1.025	4.707
50	Kentucky	11	5	6	0	0.980	1.010	4.615

Weighted Wins Standings for the Year 1989

No.	Team	G	W	L	T	IW	FW	WW
1	Colorado	11	11	0	0	1.110	1.355	10.523
2	Notre Dame	12	11	1	0	1.100	1.500	10.065
3	Tennessee	11	10	1	0	1.090	1.255	9.580
4	Michigan	11	10	1	0	1.090	1.240	9.565
5	*Miami-Florida*	*11*	*10*	*1*	*0*	*1.090*	*1.290*	*9.445*
6	Alabama	11	10	1	0	1.090	1.255	9.300
7	Nebraska	12	11	1	0	1.100	1.220	9.223
8	Virginia	12	10	2	0	1.070	1.220	9.020
9	Arkansas	11	10	1	0	1.090	1.290	8.975
10	Florida State	11	9	2	0	1.070	1.310	8.800
11	Auburn	11	9	2	0	1.070	1.210	8.775
12	Clemson	11	9	2	0	1.060	1.260	8.502
13	Illinois	11	9	2	0	1.070	1.215	8.395
14	Southern California	11	8	2	1	1.065	1.175	8.159
15	Brigham Young	12	10	2	0	1.080	1.195	8.035
16	Houston	11	9	2	0	1.070	1.145	7.950
17	West Virginia	11	8	2	1	1.065	1.172	7.654
18	Penn State	11	7	3	1	1.045	1.175	7.469
19	Texas A&M	11	8	3	0	1.050	1.120	7.400
20	Duke	10	7	3	0	1.040	1.140	7.165
21	Texas Tech	11	8	3	0	1.050	1.120	7.155
22	Hawaii	12	9	2	1	1.075	1.198	7.134
23	Ohio State	11	8	3	0	1.050	1.050	7.090
24	Air Force	12	8	3	1	1.055	1.092	6.829
25	Michigan State	11	7	4	0	1.030	1.030	6.755
26	Pittsburgh	11	7	3	1	1.045	1.097	6.656
27	Washington	11	7	4	0	1.030	1.110	6.630
28	Northern Illinois	12	9	3	0	1.040	1.060	6.382
29	South Carolina	11	6	4	1	1.015	1.097	6.349
30	Arizona	11	7	4	0	1.030	1.085	6.197
31	Mississippi	11	7	4	0	1.020	1.030	6.190
32	Georgia Tech	11	7	4	0	1.020	1.090	6.170
33	Ball State	11	7	2	2	1.050	1.097	6.145
34	North Carolina State	11	7	4	0	1.020	1.055	6.138
35	Virginia Tech	11	6	4	1	1.025	1.123	6.116
36	Oregon	11	7	4	0	1.030	1.035	6.115
37	Florida	11	7	4	0	1.030	1.040	6.065
38	Oklahoma	11	7	4	0	1.030	1.030	6.025
39	Syracuse	10	6	4	0	1.020	1.020	5.885
40	Arizona State	11	6	4	1	1.025	1.020	5.531
41	Georgia	11	6	5	0	1.010	1.050	5.442
42	Washington State	11	6	5	0	1.000	1.080	5.423
43	Colorado State	11	5	5	1	1.005	1.107	5.351
44	Fresno State	11	10	1	0	1.080	1.005	5.240
45	Kentucky	11	6	5	0	1.010	1.010	5.145
46	Texas	11	5	6	0	0.990	1.100	5.080
47	Minnesota	11	6	5	0	1.000	1.000	5.060
48	Iowa State	11	6	5	0	1.010	1.000	4.980
49	San Diego State	13	7	5	1	1.025	0.997	4.816
50	Southern Mississippi	13	7	6	0	0.990	1.010	4.720

Weighted Wins Standings for the Year 1990

No.	Team	G	W	L	T	IW	FW	WW
1	*Georgia Tech*	11	10	0	1	1.095	1.223	9.631
2	Texas	11	10	1	0	1.090	1.350	9.595
3	*Colorado*	12	10	1	1	1.095	1.410	9.545
4	Notre Dame	11	9	2	0	1.070	1.350	9.138
5	Washington	11	9	2	0	1.070	1.265	9.112
6	Penn State	11	9	2	0	1.070	1.230	8.840
7	Miami-Florida	11	9	2	0	1.070	1.255	8.760
8	Houston	11	10	1	0	1.080	1.140	8.515
9	Brigham Young	12	10	2	0	1.080	1.205	8.237
10	Florida	11	9	2	0	1.060	1.135	8.188
11	Florida State	11	9	2	0	1.060	1.130	8.085
12	Clemson	11	9	2	0	1.060	1.085	8.080
13	Michigan	11	8	3	0	1.050	1.180	8.030
14	Nebraska	11	9	2	0	1.070	1.095	7.952
15	Mississippi	11	9	2	0	1.060	1.060	7.760
16	Tennessee	12	8	2	2	1.070	1.280	7.665
17	Southern California	12	8	3	1	1.055	1.212	7.664
18	Illinois	11	8	3	0	1.040	1.240	7.570
19	Oregon	11	8	3	0	1.040	1.145	7.435
20	Iowa	11	8	3	0	1.050	1.175	7.402
21	Oklahoma	11	8	3	0	1.050	1.095	7.335
22	Southern Mississippi	11	8	3	0	1.040	1.140	7.157
23	Virginia	11	8	3	0	1.040	1.115	7.040
24	Michigan State	10	6	3	1	1.035	1.135	7.011
25	Louisville	11	9	1	1	1.065	1.092	6.979
26	Ohio State	11	7	3	1	1.045	1.117	6.906
27	Toledo	11	9	2	0	1.060	1.060	6.880
28	Auburn	11	7	3	1	1.045	1.210	6.795
29	Arizona	11	7	4	0	1.030	1.075	6.680
30	Wyoming	11	9	2	0	1.050	1.090	6.600
31	Central Michigan	11	8	2	1	1.065	1.125	6.569
32	Alabama	11	7	4	0	1.030	1.115	6.565
33	Texas A&M	12	8	3	1	1.045	1.052	6.544
34	California	11	6	4	1	1.025	1.127	6.529
35	Temple	11	7	4	0	1.020	1.030	6.178
36	Colorado State	12	8	4	0	1.030	1.010	5.835
37	Maryland	11	6	5	0	1.010	1.060	5.830
38	San Diego State	12	7	5	0	1.020	1.020	5.825
39	Stanford	12	6	6	0	1.000	1.115	5.620
40	North Carolina	11	6	4	1	1.015	1.062	5.536
41	Virginia Tech	11	6	5	0	1.010	1.090	5.523
42	Indiana	11	6	4	1	1.025	1.047	5.504
43	Baylor	11	6	4	1	1.015	1.007	5.476
44	Minnesota	11	6	5	0	1.010	1.055	5.420
45	Western Michigan	11	7	4	0	1.030	0.955	5.353
46	Syracuse	12	6	4	2	1.030	1.037	5.285
47	UCLA	11	5	6	0	0.990	1.080	5.230
48	Mississippi State	11	5	6	0	0.990	1.000	4.780
49	Air Force	12	6	6	0	0.990	1.000	4.685
50	Fresno State	11	8	2	1	1.065	1.047	4.461

Weighted Wins Standings for the Year 1991

No.	Team	G	W	L	T	IW	FW	WW
1	*Miami-Florida*	*11*	*11*	*0*	*0*	*1.110*	*1.395*	*10.688*
2	*Washington*	*11*	*11*	*0*	*0*	*1.110*	*1.330*	*10.223*
3	Florida	12	11	1	0	1.100	1.415	9.770
4	Michigan	11	10	1	0	1.090	1.325	9.355
5	Alabama	11	10	1	0	1.080	1.220	9.110
6	Florida State	12	10	2	0	1.070	1.295	9.065
7	Texas A&M	11	10	1	0	1.090	1.190	9.030
8	Nebraska	12	10	1	1	1.095	1.188	8.829
9	Iowa	11	10	1	0	1.090	1.175	8.802
10	Tennessee	11	9	2	0	1.070	1.210	8.625
11	Bowling Green	11	10	1	0	1.090	1.200	8.605
12	Penn State	12	10	2	0	1.080	1.175	8.602
13	Syracuse	11	9	2	0	1.070	1.190	8.530
14	East Carolina	11	10	1	0	1.080	1.160	8.308
15	Clemson	11	9	1	1	1.075	1.192	8.214
16	California	11	9	2	0	1.070	1.155	8.050
17	Colorado	11	8	2	1	1.065	1.163	7.661
18	Notre Dame	12	9	3	0	1.060	1.185	7.628
19	North Carolina State	11	9	2	0	1.060	1.090	7.557
20	Tulsa	11	9	2	0	1.060	1.150	7.505
21	Stanford	11	8	3	0	1.040	1.195	7.392
22	UCLA	11	8	3	0	1.050	1.170	7.355
23	Baylor	11	8	3	0	1.050	1.125	7.095
24	Oklahoma	11	8	3	0	1.040	1.040	7.032
25	Brigham Young	12	8	3	1	1.055	1.152	6.904
26	Ohio State	11	8	3	0	1.050	1.075	6.805
27	Virginia	11	8	2	1	1.055	1.113	6.761
28	San Diego State	12	8	3	1	1.055	1.103	6.564
29	Central Michigan	11	6	1	4	1.070	1.095	6.530
30	Georgia	11	8	3	0	1.040	1.105	6.522
31	Air Force	12	9	3	0	1.050	1.065	6.522
32	Mississippi State	11	7	4	0	1.030	1.020	6.245
33	Texas Christian	11	7	4	0	1.030	1.030	5.960
34	West Virginia	11	6	5	0	1.010	1.080	5.782
35	Indiana	11	6	4	1	1.025	1.025	5.671
36	Kansas State	12	7	5	0	1.000	1.010	5.620
37	North Carolina	11	7	4	0	1.020	1.020	5.583
38	Georgia Tech	12	7	5	0	1.010	1.055	5.508
39	Pittsburgh	11	6	5	0	1.010	0.990	5.430
40	Arkansas	11	6	5	0	1.010	1.030	5.425
41	Arizona State	11	6	5	0	1.010	1.000	5.348
42	Kansas	11	6	5	0	1.010	1.075	5.335
43	Illinois	11	6	5	0	1.010	1.005	5.228
44	Louisiana Tech	11	9	1	1	1.055	1.025	5.194
45	Miami-Ohio	11	6	4	1	1.025	1.020	5.132
46	Western Michigan	11	6	5	0	1.010	1.000	5.125
47	Texas Tech	11	6	5	0	1.010	1.005	4.915
48	Louisiana State	11	5	6	0	0.990	0.990	4.875
49	Toledo	11	5	5	1	1.005	0.985	4.763
50	Utah	12	7	5	0	1.020	0.995	4.757

DETERMINING THE COLLEGE FOOTBALL PLAYOFF

Weighted Wins Standings for the Year 1992

No.	Team	G	W	L	T	IW	FW	WW
1	Miami-Florida	11	11	0	0	1.100	1.350	10.355
2	*Alabama*	*12*	*12*	*0*	*0*	*1.120*	*1.315*	*10.197*
3	Texas A&M	12	12	0	0	1.120	1.190	9.755
4	Florida State	12	11	1	0	1.100	1.285	9.495
5	Notre Dame	11	9	1	1	1.085	1.302	8.949
6	Washington	11	9	2	0	1.070	1.240	8.842
7	Syracuse	11	9	2	0	1.070	1.175	8.315
8	Michigan	11	8	0	3	1.095	1.182	8.246
9	Stanford	12	9	3	0	1.060	1.245	8.130
10	Colorado	11	9	1	1	1.085	1.135	7.956
11	Hawaii	12	10	2	0	1.080	1.205	7.915
12	Nebraska	11	9	2	0	1.060	1.185	7.862
13	Bowling Green	11	9	2	0	1.070	1.220	7.852
14	Ohio State	11	8	2	1	1.065	1.242	7.594
15	North Carolina State	12	9	2	1	1.065	1.115	7.519
16	Washington State	11	8	3	0	1.040	1.185	7.502
17	Boston College	11	8	2	1	1.065	1.125	7.240
18	Georgia	11	9	2	0	1.050	1.095	7.027
19	Tennessee	11	8	3	0	1.050	1.085	6.968
20	Southern California	11	6	4	1	1.025	1.137	6.839
21	Western Michigan	10	7	2	1	1.055	1.105	6.686
22	Arizona	11	6	4	1	1.025	1.163	6.666
23	North Carolina	11	8	3	0	1.040	1.050	6.645
24	Florida	12	8	4	0	1.040	1.135	6.625
25	Brigham Young	13	9	4	0	1.050	1.170	6.510
26	Penn State	11	7	4	0	1.030	1.070	6.402
27	Fresno State	12	8	4	0	1.040	0.975	6.182
28	Toledo	10	7	3	0	1.040	1.065	6.095
29	Mississippi State	11	7	4	0	1.030	0.995	6.062
30	UCLA	11	6	5	0	1.000	1.065	6.060
31	Mississippi	11	7	4	0	1.030	1.040	6.018
32	Southern Mississippi	11	7	4	0	1.030	1.010	6.018
33	Wake Forest	11	7	4	0	1.020	1.020	5.935
34	Arizona State	11	6	5	0	1.010	1.035	5.902
35	Kansas	11	7	4	0	1.030	0.960	5.817
36	Oregon	12	6	5	1	1.015	1.077	5.609
37	Auburn	11	6	4	1	1.015	1.075	5.556
38	Akron	11	7	3	1	1.040	1.020	5.520
39	Rutgers	11	7	4	0	1.020	0.990	5.497
40	West Virginia	11	5	4	2	1.020	1.065	5.415
41	Virginia	12	7	5	0	1.010	1.010	5.367
42	Miami-Ohio	11	6	4	1	1.025	1.080	5.242
43	Illinois	11	6	4	1	1.025	0.967	5.164
44	Air Force	12	7	5	0	1.020	1.005	5.067
45	San Diego State	11	5	5	1	1.005	1.127	5.059
46	Utah	11	6	5	0	1.010	0.970	5.045
47	Texas	11	6	5	0	1.000	0.965	5.020
48	Baylor	11	6	5	0	1.010	1.000	5.010
49	Oklahoma	11	5	4	2	1.020	1.062	4.860
50	Michigan State	11	5	6	0	0.990	0.990	4.695

Weighted Wins Standings for the Year 1993

No.	Team	G	W	L	T	IW	FW	WW
1	West Virginia	11	11	0	0	1.110	1.345	10.232
2	Nebraska	11	11	0	0	1.100	1.310	10.185
3	Auburn	11	11	0	0	1.100	1.250	10.055
4	*Florida State*	*12*	*11*	*1*	*0*	*1.100*	*1.410*	*9.860*
5	Notre Dame	11	10	1	0	1.090	1.270	9.610
6	Ohio State	11	9	1	1	1.085	1.298	8.924
7	Texas A&M	11	10	1	0	1.090	1.155	8.877
8	Florida	12	10	2	0	1.080	1.300	8.817
9	Miami-Florida	11	9	2	0	1.060	1.240	8.795
10	Tennessee	11	9	1	1	1.085	1.197	8.636
11	Wisconsin	11	9	1	1	1.085	1.198	8.604
12	Penn State	11	9	2	0	1.070	1.170	8.402
13	Arizona	11	9	2	0	1.070	1.100	8.060
14	North Carolina	12	10	2	0	1.080	1.160	7.980
15	UCLA	11	8	3	0	1.050	1.180	7.655
16	Virginia Tech	11	8	3	0	1.050	1.145	7.463
17	Boston College	11	8	3	0	1.050	1.145	7.462
18	Kansas State	11	8	2	1	1.055	1.077	7.249
19	Louisville	11	8	3	0	1.050	1.075	7.155
20	Oklahoma	11	8	3	0	1.050	1.145	7.147
21	Indiana	11	8	3	0	1.050	1.080	7.090
22	Colorado	11	7	3	1	1.045	1.097	6.901
23	Michigan State	10	6	4	0	1.020	1.060	6.790
24	Michigan	11	7	4	0	1.030	1.185	6.780
25	Ball State	11	8	2	1	1.055	1.075	6.722
26	Clemson	11	8	3	0	1.040	1.010	6.720
27	Alabama	12	8	3	1	1.055	1.092	6.711
28	Fresno State	11	8	3	0	1.050	1.050	6.705
29	Cincinnati	12	9	3	0	1.050	1.085	6.603
30	Washington	11	7	4	0	1.030	1.070	6.383
31	California	12	8	4	0	1.040	1.140	6.285
32	Virginia	11	7	4	0	1.030	1.110	6.095
33	Syracuse	11	6	4	1	1.025	1.132	6.094
34	Southern California	12	7	5	0	1.020	1.090	5.985
35	North Carolina State	11	7	4	0	1.020	1.010	5.970
36	Louisiana-Lafayette	11	8	3	0	1.050	1.030	5.925
37	Georgia	11	6	5	0	1.010	1.010	5.513
38	Bowling Green	11	6	3	2	1.040	1.080	5.475
39	Wyoming	11	8	3	0	1.040	1.070	5.470
40	Arizona State	11	6	5	0	1.010	1.080	5.370
41	Brigham Young	11	6	5	0	1.010	1.010	5.260
42	Kentucky	12	7	5	0	1.020	0.990	5.170
43	Iowa	11	6	5	0	1.010	1.000	5.135
44	Texas Tech	11	6	5	0	1.010	1.005	5.047
45	Louisiana State	11	5	6	0	0.990	1.055	4.977
46	Arkansas	11	5	5	1	1.005	0.975	4.901
47	Rice	11	6	5	0	1.000	0.990	4.880
48	Illinois	11	5	6	0	0.990	0.975	4.820
49	Memphis	11	6	5	0	1.010	0.990	4.792
50	Texas	11	5	5	1	1.005	1.017	4.754

Weighted Wins Standings for the Year 1994

No.	Team	G	W	L	T	IW	FW	WW
1	Penn State	11	11	0	0	1.110	1.275	10.485
2	*Nebraska*	*12*	*12*	*0*	*0*	*1.110*	*1.310*	*10.280*
3	Miami-Florida	11	10	1	0	1.080	1.295	9.552
4	Texas A&M	11	10	0	1	1.105	1.225	9.539
5	Alabama	12	11	1	0	1.090	1.270	9.497
6	Florida State	11	9	1	1	1.085	1.337	9.424
7	Florida	12	10	1	1	1.095	1.292	9.139
8	Colorado	11	10	1	0	1.090	1.255	9.135
9	Colorado State	11	10	1	0	1.090	1.240	8.745
10	Auburn	11	9	1	1	1.075	1.252	8.539
11	Kansas State	11	9	2	0	1.070	1.100	7.880
12	Utah	11	9	2	0	1.060	1.240	7.680
13	Bowling Green	11	9	2	0	1.070	1.085	7.612
14	Central Michigan	11	9	2	0	1.070	1.180	7.530
15	Virginia Tech	11	8	3	0	1.050	1.120	7.415
16	Ohio State	12	9	3	0	1.060	1.125	7.405
17	Virginia	11	8	3	0	1.040	1.140	7.328
18	Oregon	12	9	3	0	1.050	1.125	7.297
19	North Carolina State	11	8	3	0	1.040	1.200	7.292
20	Duke	11	8	3	0	1.050	1.110	7.247
21	North Carolina	11	8	3	0	1.050	1.150	7.185
22	Brigham Young	12	9	3	0	1.060	1.075	6.987
23	Southern California	11	7	3	1	1.045	1.188	6.954
24	Michigan	11	7	4	0	1.030	1.095	6.925
25	Arizona	11	8	3	0	1.050	1.080	6.917
26	Mississippi State	11	8	3	0	1.050	1.070	6.907
27	Tennessee	11	7	4	0	1.030	1.095	6.555
28	Washington State	11	7	4	0	1.030	1.080	6.398
29	Syracuse	11	7	4	0	1.030	1.105	6.367
30	Washington	11	7	4	0	1.030	1.135	6.337
31	Texas	11	7	4	0	1.030	1.100	6.173
32	East Carolina	11	7	4	0	1.020	1.040	6.160
33	Notre Dame	11	6	4	1	1.025	1.087	6.124
34	Air Force	12	8	4	0	1.040	1.065	6.062
35	Texas Christian	11	7	4	0	1.030	1.040	5.933
36	Oklahoma	11	6	5	0	1.010	1.050	5.930
37	Wisconsin	11	6	4	1	1.025	1.005	5.902
38	Boston College	11	6	4	1	1.025	1.092	5.901
39	Baylor	11	7	4	0	1.030	1.060	5.755
40	West Virginia	12	7	5	0	1.020	1.050	5.717
41	Georgia	11	6	4	1	1.025	1.062	5.709
42	Illinois	11	6	5	0	1.010	1.075	5.460
43	Southern Mississippi	11	6	5	0	1.000	1.020	5.373
44	Indiana	11	6	5	0	1.010	0.975	5.347
45	Texas Tech	11	6	5	0	1.010	1.070	5.268
46	South Carolina	11	6	5	0	1.010	1.010	5.225
47	Iowa	11	5	5	1	1.005	1.075	5.177
48	Kansas	11	6	5	0	1.000	1.000	5.145
49	Rutgers	11	5	5	1	1.005	0.987	4.949
50	Western Michigan	11	7	4	0	1.020	1.025	4.935

Weighted Wins Standings for the Year 1995

No.	Team	G	W	L	T	IW	FW	WW
1	Florida	12	12	0	0	1.120	1.395	10.518
2	*Nebraska*	*11*	*11*	*0*	*0*	*1.100*	*1.360*	*10.407*
3	Northwestern	11	10	1	0	1.090	1.335	10.125
4	Ohio State	12	11	1	0	1.100	1.290	9.960
5	Tennessee	11	10	1	0	1.090	1.250	9.222
6	Toledo	11	10	0	1	1.095	1.248	9.196
7	Notre Dame	11	9	2	0	1.070	1.315	8.925
8	Texas	12	10	1	1	1.095	1.263	8.761
9	Colorado	11	9	2	0	1.070	1.235	8.603
10	Kansas	11	9	2	0	1.070	1.175	8.393
11	Kansas State	11	9	2	0	1.070	1.165	8.172
12	Michigan	12	9	3	0	1.060	1.260	8.140
13	Florida State	11	9	2	0	1.070	1.170	8.125
14	Oregon	11	9	2	0	1.060	1.170	8.043
15	Penn State	11	8	3	0	1.050	1.205	7.828
16	Miami-Ohio	11	8	2	1	1.065	1.232	7.644
17	Southern California	11	8	2	1	1.065	1.142	7.621
18	Virginia Tech	11	9	2	0	1.070	1.150	7.585
19	Washington	11	7	3	1	1.045	1.162	7.421
20	Alabama	11	8	3	0	1.050	1.095	7.105
21	Texas A&M	11	8	3	0	1.040	1.105	7.033
22	East Carolina	11	8	3	0	1.050	1.110	6.925
23	Miami-Florida	11	8	3	0	1.040	1.120	6.910
24	Colorado State	11	8	3	0	1.040	1.120	6.895
25	Syracuse	11	8	3	0	1.050	1.080	6.890
26	Auburn	11	8	3	0	1.040	1.120	6.885
27	Texas Tech	11	8	3	0	1.050	1.100	6.798
28	Stanford	11	7	3	1	1.045	1.145	6.773
29	Clemson	11	8	3	0	1.040	1.060	6.757
30	Virginia	12	8	4	0	1.030	1.150	6.692
31	UCLA	11	7	4	0	1.030	1.150	6.660
32	Iowa	11	7	4	0	1.020	1.045	6.645
33	Air Force	12	8	4	0	1.040	1.080	6.475
34	Michigan State	11	6	4	1	1.025	1.120	6.404
35	Arkansas	12	8	4	0	1.040	1.040	6.363
36	Brigham Young	11	7	4	0	1.030	1.120	6.360
37	Utah	11	7	4	0	1.030	1.110	6.285
38	Nevada	11	9	2	0	1.060	1.060	6.207
39	San Diego State	12	8	4	0	1.040	1.130	5.983
40	Oklahoma	10	5	4	1	1.015	1.103	5.951
41	Baylor	11	7	4	0	1.030	1.040	5.937
42	Arizona State	11	6	5	0	1.010	1.130	5.900
43	Illinois	11	5	5	1	1.005	1.075	5.817
44	Louisiana State	11	6	4	1	1.025	1.075	5.724
45	Cincinnati	11	6	5	0	1.010	1.110	5.695
46	Georgia	11	6	5	0	1.010	1.050	5.668
47	Western Michigan	11	7	4	0	1.020	0.970	5.402
48	Louisville	11	7	4	0	1.030	1.040	5.325
49	Mississippi	11	6	5	0	1.000	1.010	5.295
50	Wisconsin	11	4	5	2	1.000	1.085	5.257

Weighted Wins Standings for the Year 1996

No.	Team	G	W	L	IW	FW	WW
1	Florida State	11	11	0	1.110	1.410	10.670
2	Arizona State	11	11	0	1.110	1.290	10.310
3	*Florida*	*12*	*11*	*1*	*1.090*	*1.330*	*9.660*
4	Ohio State	11	10	1	1.090	1.320	9.580
5	Virginia Tech	11	10	1	1.090	1.250	9.150
6	Brigham Young	14	13	1	1.120	1.280	9.150
7	Washington	11	9	2	1.070	1.210	8.580
8	Penn State	12	10	2	1.080	1.230	8.500
9	North Carolina	11	9	2	1.070	1.160	8.480
10	Nebraska	12	10	2	1.080	1.260	8.430
11	Colorado	11	9	2	1.070	1.180	8.370
12	Tennessee	11	9	2	1.070	1.110	8.130
13	Northwestern	11	9	2	1.070	1.130	8.100
14	Louisiana State	11	9	2	1.070	1.120	8.090
15	Kansas State	11	9	2	1.060	1.130	7.980
16	Army	11	10	1	1.070	1.130	7.690
17	Wyoming	12	10	2	1.080	1.100	7.690
18	Michigan	11	8	3	1.050	1.170	7.590
19	Miami-Florida	11	8	3	1.040	1.140	7.550
20	Southern Mississippi	11	8	3	1.050	1.100	7.500
21	Notre Dame	11	8	3	1.050	1.200	7.450
22	Syracuse	11	8	3	1.050	1.230	7.380
23	Iowa	11	8	3	1.050	1.130	7.330
24	Alabama	12	9	3	1.060	1.200	7.240
25	East Carolina	11	8	3	1.040	1.090	7.060
26	West Virginia	11	8	3	1.050	1.090	7.030
27	Utah	11	8	3	1.050	1.060	6.980
28	Navy	11	8	3	1.040	1.030	6.750
29	San Diego State	11	8	3	1.050	1.040	6.570
30	Virginia	11	7	4	1.030	1.130	6.570
31	Rice	11	7	4	1.030	1.080	6.460
32	Texas	12	8	4	1.040	1.100	6.350
33	Auburn	11	7	4	1.030	1.030	6.260
34	Texas Tech	11	7	4	1.030	1.020	6.160
35	Ball State	11	8	3	1.050	1.010	6.110
36	Houston	11	7	4	1.020	1.070	6.090
37	Clemson	11	7	4	1.020	1.040	6.070
38	Stanford	11	6	5	1.010	0.960	5.510
39	Oregon	11	6	5	1.010	1.050	5.500
40	Michigan State	11	6	5	1.010	1.020	5.480
41	Wisconsin	12	7	5	1.020	1.030	5.400
42	South Carolina	11	6	5	1.010	1.020	5.350
43	Colorado State	12	7	5	1.010	1.040	5.320
44	Air Force	11	6	5	1.010	1.090	5.250
45	Nevada	11	8	3	1.040	1.020	5.250
46	California	11	6	5	1.010	1.080	5.250
47	Southern California	12	6	6	1.000	1.060	5.020
48	UCLA	11	5	6	0.990	1.000	4.970
49	Cincinnati	11	6	5	1.010	0.920	4.940
50	Toledo	11	7	4	1.020	0.970	4.830

Weighted Wins Standings for the Year 1997

No.	Team	G	W	L	IW	FW	WW
1	*Michigan*	*11*	*11*	*0*	*1.110*	*1.370*	*10.570*
2	*Nebraska*	*12*	*12*	*0*	*1.120*	*1.330*	*10.320*
3	Tennessee	12	11	1	1.100	1.390	10.200
4	Florida State	11	10	1	1.090	1.250	9.600
5	Kansas State	11	10	1	1.090	1.220	9.280
6	Florida	11	9	2	1.070	1.370	9.170
7	North Carolina	11	10	1	1.090	1.150	9.020
8	Georgia	11	9	2	1.070	1.210	8.930
9	Washington State	11	10	1	1.090	1.220	8.930
10	Ohio State	12	10	2	1.080	1.170	8.600
11	UCLA	11	9	2	1.070	1.130	8.500
12	Auburn	12	9	3	1.060	1.300	8.310
13	Penn State	11	9	2	1.070	1.250	8.230
14	Colorado State	12	10	2	1.080	1.120	7.780
15	Louisiana State	11	8	3	1.050	1.150	7.720
16	Marshall	12	10	2	1.070	1.170	7.590
17	Air Force	12	10	2	1.070	1.150	7.340
18	Purdue	11	8	3	1.050	1.140	7.290
19	Louisiana Tech	11	9	2	1.070	1.040	7.230
20	Southern Mississippi	11	8	3	1.050	1.080	7.230
21	Arizona State	11	8	3	1.050	1.160	7.210
22	Mississippi	11	7	4	1.030	1.120	7.070
23	Syracuse	12	9	3	1.060	1.130	7.070
24	Toledo	12	9	3	1.060	1.170	6.920
25	Washington	11	7	4	1.030	1.110	6.840
26	Texas A&M	12	9	3	1.050	1.100	6.740
27	Miami-Ohio	11	8	3	1.050	1.140	6.720
28	Mississippi State	11	7	4	1.030	1.060	6.610
29	Virginia	11	7	4	1.020	1.080	6.610
30	Michigan State	11	7	4	1.030	1.150	6.580
31	New Mexico	12	9	3	1.050	1.070	6.550
32	Ohio University	11	8	3	1.040	1.090	6.490
33	Wisconsin	12	8	4	1.040	1.060	6.420
34	Oklahoma State	11	8	3	1.050	1.050	6.410
35	Western Michigan	11	8	3	1.050	1.050	6.370
36	Missouri	11	7	4	1.030	1.070	6.260
37	Clemson	11	7	4	1.020	1.030	6.210
38	West Virginia	11	7	4	1.030	1.100	6.130
39	Rice	11	7	4	1.030	1.090	5.980
40	Notre Dame	12	7	5	1.020	1.120	5.850
41	Southern California	11	6	5	1.010	1.040	5.840
42	Iowa	11	7	4	1.020	1.050	5.810
43	Virginia Tech	11	7	4	1.030	1.090	5.770
44	Georgia Tech	11	6	5	1.010	1.040	5.730
45	Tulane	11	7	4	1.030	1.060	5.710
46	Cincinnati	11	7	4	1.030	1.020	5.690
47	Arizona	11	6	5	1.010	1.060	5.660
48	Oregon	11	6	5	1.010	1.050	5.610
49	South Carolina	11	5	6	0.990	0.990	5.460
50	North Carolina State	11	6	5	1.010	1.080	5.390

ABOUT THE AUTHORS

Ray D. Theis is a retired college mathematics professor, having taught at the university level for thirty years. During his career, he taught students at all levels, from the second grade through the doctoral level. As a high school teacher, he coached and officiated both football and basketball. His broad teaching experience, coupled with his passion for fairness of process, motivated him to develop the system of Weighted Wins, which had its second copyright revision in 2004. His goal was to create a system that is fair, consistent, unbiased, and understandable. As a seventy-year college football fan, Ray loves the college football playoffs but would like to see a better selection process.

Mark G. Terwilliger is a computer science professor at the University of North Alabama. Whether it is playing, coaching, officiating, or watching sports, he is a self-admitted sports junkie. A native Michigander, Mark previously coached tennis and basketball at Lake Superior State University, where his real job was a professor of computer science and mathematics. A former college tennis player, he is a big follower of college football, as well as a die-hard fan of his Detroit Lions, Pistons, Tigers, and Red Wings. As someone who loves to code, Mark used his programming background to move Weighted Wins from a great idea to a working software system.